THE ART OF THINKING IN GRAPHS

Illustrating the 52 Principles That Shape
Our Productivity, Decision-Making, and
the Way We Think

Production by eBookPro Publishing
www.ebook-pro.com

THE ART OF THINKING IN GRAPHS
Dolev Erez

Copyright ©2025 Dolev Erez

All rights reserved; no parts of this book may be reproduced or transmitted in any form or by any means, electronic or mechanical, including photocopying, recording, taping, or by any information retrieval system, without the permission, in writing, of the author.

Editing: lilach.shahar
Contact: 52Graphs@gmail.com

ISBN 9798303500631

Contents

PREFACE 7
How to Navigate "The Art of Thinking in Graphs" 10
Unpacking The Chapter Structure 12

PART 1: Your Graphical Beginning 13
Chapter 1: The Dunning-Kruger Effect................................... 14
Chapter 2: The Flow State.. 19
Chapter 3: Loss Aversion..24
Chapter 4: The Lindy Effect...29
Chapter 5: The Imposter Syndrome....................................... 35

PART 2: The Fundamental Graphs 37
Chapter 6: The Pareto's Law (The 80/20 Principle) 38
Chapter 7: The Law of Diminishing Returns 43
Chapter 8: Compound Interest 48
Chapter 9: Cognitive Dissonance..54
Chapter 10: Emotional Cycle of Change................................59
Chapter 11: The Forgetting Curve...64
Chapter 12: The Gaussian Distribution 69
Chapter 13: Stigler's Law of Eponymy 74
Chapter 14: The Baader-Meinhof Phenomenon................... 79

PART 3: The Social and Organizational Graphs 81
Chapter 15: The Rosenthal Effect (Pygmalion Effect).......... 82
Chapter 16: The Matthew Effect... 87

Chapter 17: The Peter Principle 92
Chapter 18: The Milgram Obedience Experiment 97
Chapter 19: The Bystander Effect 102
Chapter 20: The Hawthorne Effect 106
Chapter 21: The Streisand Effect 110
Chapter 22: The Spotlight Effect 115
Chapter 23: The Spotlight Effect Through Life's Stages 120

PART 4: The Decision-Making Graphs 123
Chapter 24: The Sunk Cost Fallacy 124
Chapter 25: The Decision Fatigue 129
Chapter 26: Hick's Law 134
Chapter 27: The Scarcity Principle 139
Chapter 28: Fredkin's Paradox 143
Chapter 29: The Endowment Effect 147
Chapter 30: The Balance of Heart and Mind 152

PART 5: The Emotional Graphs 155
Chapter 31: The Hedonic Treadmill 156
Chapter 32: The Happiness-Income Correlation 160
Chapter 33: The Kübler-Ross Model 165
Chapter 34: The Romantic Fantasy Effect 169
Chapter 35: The Ben Franklin Effect 174
Chapter 36: The Hedgehog's Dilemma 179
Chapter 37: The Power of Asking 183

PART 6: The Productivity Graphs 185
Chapter 38: Parkinson's Law 186
Chapter 39: The Yerkes-Dodson Law 191
Chapter 40: Life's Friction 196
Chapter 41: The Over-Justification Effect 200

Chapter 42: The Zeigarnik Effect 204
Chapter 43: The Red Queen Hypothesis............................. 208
Chapter 44: The Incremental Triumphs Framework 213
Chapter 45: The Reflection Ripple Effect 217

PART 7: The Advanced Graphs................................... 219
Chapter 46: Life's 3 Ages 220
Chapter 47: The Law of Truly Large Numbers 224
Chapter 48: The Wisdom of Crowds 228
Chapter 49: The Flynn Effect..232
Chapter 50: Dunbar's Number...237
Chapter 51: The Comeback Mindset 241
Chapter 52: Life is All About Wins and Lessons 245

Graphical Independence: A Lifelong Tool...........................247

References.. 248

PREFACE

Welcome to "The Art of Thinking in Graphs," a journey to unravel the mysteries of existence through the simplicity of graphs. As you turn the pages of this book, you will gain accessible and intuitive knowledge about the patterns that govern our behavior, decisions, emotions, productivity, society and more.

This book is more than just a collection of axes, lines, and points; it is a visual toolkit crafted meticulously to enhance the understanding of the world around us. More than theoretical knowledge, each chapter concludes with practical insights, enabling you to apply its lessons to enhance your well-being and manage your day-to-day activities more effectively.

Why This Book Matters

"The Art of Thinking in Graphs" is a testament to the beauty of simplicity and the power of visual learning. Through a collection of elegantly simple line graphs, it distills complex principles that can fill entire books (and indeed, some already have) into few concise pages with accessible life insights, offering a unique lens to view and understand the world around us. It's a visual journey that transcends traditional text, making profound concepts more tangible and memorable.

The Birth of the Idea

Throughout my twenties, I stumbled upon a cognitive phenomenon which I found both fascinating and profoundly applicable to everyday life: the Dunning-Kruger effect (rest assured, the full exploration of this intriguing effect awaits you in the very first chapter). Remarkably, I discovered that this effect has a very simple, yet highly accurate graphical representation that beautifully illustrates the concept. This discovery sparked my journey to uncover more of these visual treasures. Over the following years, my collection grew, with each graph offering a unique insight into the laws and effects that shape our reality. Finally, the idea of creating a book turned into reality, culminating in "The Art of Thinking in Graphs."

A Note of Clarity

Some graphs are general representations, crafted intentionally to convey the underlying message more clearly. These general representations are not meant to be precise replicas of original scientific data, but rather tools to enhance clarity and facilitate a better understanding of the different concepts in each chapter.

A Glimpse into the Future

As you explore these pages, you'll encounter intriguing concepts like the Red Queen Hypothesis, the Streisand Effect, and the Over-Justification Effect. Surprisingly, some concepts may even apply to the book itself, like Stigler's Law of Eponymy, which highlights that no idea or discovery is typically named after its original discoverer. Therefore, maybe one day my book will be known by another name, but that's the beauty of knowledge – it's a shared treasure.

Final Piece of Advice

Remember that each graph is a general illustration of life's endless situations. Factors like the graph's slope, starting and ending point, the vertical and horizontal scales, and other parameters can shape a completely different story. At the end of each chapter, take a moment to contemplate these factors. What influences might alter the graph's course? How do these variations resonate with your own experiences? Engaging with these questions will not only deepen your comprehension but also empower you to apply these insights to your personal growth journey.

How to Navigate
"The Art of Thinking in Graphs"

Before diving into the chapters, I strongly recommend taking the time to read this guide thoroughly. It will give you a clear understanding of the book's purpose, structure and how to get the most value out of it.

Overview of the Book's Structure

The book is divided into seven parts, each focusing on a different subject. The order of these parts is designed to guide you through a logical progression of ideas, starting with the fundamental concepts in the second part and gradually building towards more complex and advanced topics.

Part 1 – Your Graphical Beginning: Kickstart your adventure with several intriguing principles from various subjects featured in the book. This is your first encounter with the captivating blend of graphical representation and the laws of life.

Part 2 – The Fundamental Graphs: Dive into the core principles that govern various aspects of life. Pay close attention to these key graphs, as they will reappear in later chapters to illustrate for us the interconnectedness of life's principles across different topics in life.

Part 3 – The Social and Organizational Graphs: Explore the complexities of society, business, and education by understanding the forces that drive human interaction.

Part 4 – The Decision-Making Graphs: Navigate into the intricacies of decision-making, exploring cognitive biases, and mental processes.

Part 5 – The Emotional Graphs: Delve into the heart's depths, exploring emotions like happiness, sadness, and love, and their profound impact on our lives.

Part 6 – The Productivity Graphs: Discover effective strategies to enhance productivity and management skills, paving the way for a more fulfilling and successful life.

Part 7 – The Advanced Graphs: Venture into the realm of life's mysteries, where advanced and theoretical ideas will challenge your understanding and provoke deep reflection.

Interactive Chapters: At the end of each part, engage with thought-provoking and shorter principles that challenge your understanding and encourage personal growth. While these concepts may not have the same level of scientific backing as others in the book, they offer valuable opportunities for introspection and self-discovery. Approach these chapters with an open mind, ready to explore new ideas and gain fresh perspectives on your own life experiences.

Unpacking The Chapter Structure

Each chapter follows a consistent format to facilitate understanding and application:

Quote: A short quote that captures the core idea of the chapter's principle. *Some quotes are attributed to their authors, while others are my own creations and are presented without any attribution.*

Principle Introduction: A brief overview of the principle, outlining its importance and impact in everyday life.

Graphical Representation: The visual representation of the principle.

Graphical Key Points: A concise explanation of the most important points in the graph.

Life Scenario: Real-life example that illustrates the principle.

Wider Implications: Diverse applications of the principle across different areas of life.

Principle Origins: Historical background or foundational research that led to the principle's formulation.

Analyzing the Principle: An in-depth examination of the underlying reasons behind the principle, shedding light on its true causes.

Insights to Implement in Life: Practical takeaways or lessons that you can apply in life based on the principle.

Summary: Concise overview of the main concepts and insights discussed in the chapter.

Part 1
Your Graphical Beginning

"A good sketch is better than a long speech."

– Napoleon Bonaparte

This part is your gateway to a deeper understanding of your life, setting the stage for the rich exploration that lies ahead. Here, there are a few single chapters on different topics, such as behavioral biases, decision-making, and productivity, which serve as a preview for the more detailed later parts of the book. So, let's turn the page and start this adventure together, with open minds and ignited curiosity, ready to uncover the secrets of life one graph at a time. Good luck!

Chapter 1: The Dunning-Kruger Effect

"The first rule of the Dunning-Kruger club is you don't know you're a member of the Dunning-Kruger club."

– David Dunning

Principle Introduction:

In our first chapter, we begin where my journey into the graphical exploration of life's principles started: The Dunning-Kruger Effect, which illustrates a cognitive bias where individuals with limited knowledge or progress in a domain significantly overestimate their abilities, while experts tend to underestimate theirs, often unknowingly.

Graphical Representation:

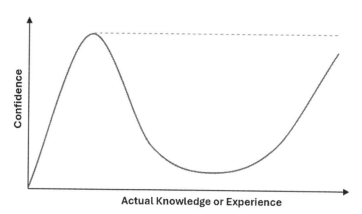

Graphical Key Points:

- **"The Initial Overconfidence"** – High confidence with limited knowledge.

- **"The Valley of Realization"** – Decrease in confidence while gaining more knowledge.
- **"The Ascend to Justified Confidence"** – Confidence grows with increasing expertise (although not as much as the initial confidence).

Life Scenario:

A novice cook feels confident after mastering a few simple recipes and decides to host a large dinner party. However, when faced with the complexities of timing, seasoning, and presentation for multiple dishes, his initial confidence is shaken. This experience serves as a wake-up call, leading to a humbler approach and a deeper commitment to learning the culinary arts.

Wider Implications:

- **Driving:** Drivers tend to overestimate their driving skills, with studies showing that around 85-90% of drivers believe they are above average.
- **Workplace Dynamics:** Employees who overestimate their abilities may take on tasks or roles they are not fully prepared for, leading to poor work performance and potential setbacks in their career.
- **Social Interactions:** Individuals who overestimate their social skills may struggle to read social cues, leading to awkward or inappropriate interactions.

Principle Origins:

The Dunning-Kruger Effect was first identified by psychologists David Dunning and Justin Kruger in their seminal 1999 study, inspired by an unusual event involving a bank robber named McArthur Wheeler. Wheeler, believing that covering his face with lemon juice would render him invisible to surveillance cameras, confidently committed a robbery without any disguise. When caught, his bewildered reaction to being identified led Dunning and Kruger to explore the cognitive bias that now bears their names. They conducted a series of experiments where participants were asked to perform tasks in areas such as humor, logic, and grammar. After completing the tests, participants were asked to estimate their performance. The results consistently showed that those who performed poorly often grossly overestimated their abilities, while those with high performance tended to underestimate their skills. This stark contrast between self-perception and actual ability led to the conceptualization of the Dunning-Kruger Effect, visualized in the graph that depicts this phenomenon.

Analyzing the Principle:

- **Cognitive Inadequacy:** Individuals with limited knowledge or experience in a specific domain often lack the necessary cognitive tools to recognize their own incompetence. This lack of self-awareness leads to an inflated sense of self-assessment. This isn't ignorance, but a misplaced belief in their own competence.
- **Expert Humility:** Experienced individuals in a field are often acutely aware of the vastness of their domain and the limits of their own knowledge. This awareness leads them to adopt a more cautious approach in evaluating their own abilities. This isn't a lack of confidence, but a realistic assessment of their skills in the context of the broader landscape of their field.
- **Early Wins vs. Lasting Skills:** Early successes may not

always translate into deep expertise but often only due to sheer luck. This misinterpretation of success results in an overestimation of one's skills and abilities.

Insights to Implement in Life:

- **Valuing Failure:** Recognize that sometimes it takes a significant failure to reveal the extent of our overconfidence and our actual location on the graph. Such moments, while humbling, are invaluable – they mark the transition from illusion to enlightenment on our journey.
- **Navigating the Valley of Desperation:** When you find yourself in the depths of the Valley of Desperation (even not after a particular failure), it's a critical turning point in your learning journey. This is not the moment to retreat but the moment to understand that you are about halfway through. Remember, everyone who got good at something went through this tough time too. Keep going, and you'll get better just like they did.
- **Initial Confidence Fuels Beginnings:** Just like a child's grand dreams pave the path for their future achievements, early confidence in learning is the spark that ignites action. This burst of enthusiasm is crucial – it sets you in motion, taking the first steps that many hesitate to start. Even if confidence diminishes later, remember that it was this initial stage that launched your journey toward mastery.

Summary:

The Dunning-Kruger Effect is not just a line on a graph – it's the narrative of our growth from overconfident novices to realistic experts. By embracing this understanding, we can navigate our skills and knowledge with humility and strive for true proficiency. Let this chapter serve as a mirror to reflect on our learning journey, reminding us that every expert was once a beginner.

A personal tip from me: Some of the upcoming chapters may contain complex concepts that need some time to fully sink in. If you find yourself feeling confident that you've understood these chapters after just one read, I encourage you to revisit the opening quote of this chapter, as you might have unknowingly joined the Dunning-Kruger club.

Chapter 2: The Flow State

"Skills and challenge, in sync, create flow."

Principle Introduction:

In this chapter, we explore how the balance between skill and challenge affects our productivity. When challenges overwhelm skills, we enter "The Anxiety Zone," leading to stress and frustration. Conversely, when skills exceed challenges, we slip into "The Boredom Zone," resulting in disengagement and apathy. The sweet spot, known as the Flow State, arises when the level of challenge perfectly matches our level of skill, igniting intense focus and unlocking a profound sense of fulfillment.

Graphical Representation:

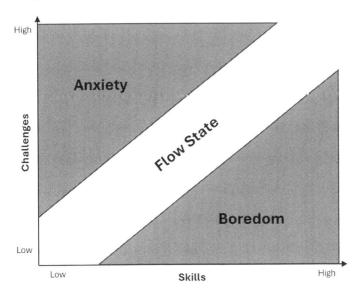

Graphical Key Points:

- **"The Anxiety Zone"** – A zone where challenges overwhelm skills, leading to stress.
- **"The Boredom Zone"** – A zone where skills exceed challenges, resulting in disengagement.
- **"The Flow State"** – Depicting the journey of increasing challenges and skills in harmony.

Life Scenario:

Imagine you start a new office job where the first tasks match your skill level, keeping you engaged and productive. As time goes on, you're given a difficult project with tight deadlines, and you start to feel overwhelmed and stressed. This is the Anxiety Zone, where the challenge exceeds your current abilities. Over time, you master your tasks and find the routine work unchallenging, leading to boredom and disengagement in the Boredom Zone. To achieve the Flow State, seek out new responsibilities and projects that are slightly more challenging. This will align your skills with these new tasks, fostering intense focus and job satisfaction.

Wider Implications:

- **Parenting:** Parents can encourage their children's growth by providing activities that are appropriately challenging, promoting engagement and development without causing undue frustration or boredom.
- **Personal Habits:** When forming new habits, individuals can maintain motivation by setting goals that are slightly beyond their current capabilities. For instance, gradually increasing the intensity of a workout routine

can help sustain engagement and ensure continuous improvement without causing burnout.
- **Education:** Designing lessons that align with students' abilities, promoting optimal learning and engagement.

Principle Origins:

The genesis of the Flow Model can be traced back to the 1960s when Hungarian-American psychologist Mihaly Csikszentmihalyi began studying artists who would become utterly absorbed in their work, to the point of excluding all other distractions. Over a period of 12 years, he researched what he termed "flow," discovering that this highly focused mental state wasn't exclusive to artists, but a universal experience that could be achieved across all kinds of activities. His work laid the foundations for the positive psychology movement, affirming that flow can significantly enrich one's life and is accessible to nearly everyone with the right balance of challenge and skill.

Analyzing the Principle:

- **Immediate Feedback Loop:** A defining feature of the flow state is the feedback loop, which is knowing instantly how well you are doing. When immersed in an activity, immediate feedback helps adjust performance on the fly, which reinforces a sense of control and mastery. This feedback doesn't have to come from an external source, it can also be internal, as in when you just "know" you're performing well.
- **Exploring New Challenges:** The Flow State graph illuminates our progress in different experiences. For example, when attempting a new recipe, the challenge

is considerable and exciting at the beginning, and therefore aligns well with our abilities to enter the flow state. As we repeat the same dish, our skill increases, and the challenge decreases, potentially leading to a dip below the flow state into boredom. This natural progression motivates us to pursue new, more complex recipes to re-enter the flow state, continuously pushing our boundaries and fostering growth.
- **Group Flow:** Group flow occurs when the flow state extends beyond the individual and takes root within a group. This can be seen in scenarios like a well-coordinated basketball team, where each player's individual focus and immersion are synchronized with the team's overall rhythm. For group flow to emerge, clear communication and shared goals are essential. When everyone's personal flow states interconnect, the group becomes a cohesive, productive, and creative unit.

Insights to Implement in Life:

- **Seek Challenges Slightly Above your Skill Level:** This strategy keeps you engaged and growing without causing anxiety. By gradually pushing your comfort zone, you'll continuously improve and expand your potential. This approach ensures manageable progress and cultivates resilience, essential for success in any endeavor.
- **Contemplate on Your Emotional State:** Regularly assess your emotional state and level of engagement in various activities. By recognizing when you're in the Flow Zone, Anxiety Zone, or Boredom Zone, you can make proactive decisions to adjust your tasks or

mindset accordingly. This heightened self-awareness allows you to optimize your experiences and maintain a sense of balance.
- **Understand Your Flow Signs:** Learn to recognize when you're deeply immersed in an activity and time flows differently. These are indicators of flow. Noting these experiences will help you craft a conducive environment to enter this optimal state in the future.

Summary:

The Flow State is a deeply rewarding experience where individuals perform activities at their highest level of competence, which enhances fulfillment in key areas such as work, relationships, and personal development. By understanding and applying Csikszentmihalyi's Flow Model, you can seek to replicate this optimal experience across various facets of life.

Chapter 3: Loss Aversion

"The concept of loss aversion is certainly the most significant contribution of psychology to behavioral economics."

– Daniel Kahneman

Principle Introduction:

Loss aversion is a key concept in decision-making that highlights our innate tendency to prioritize avoiding losses over acquiring gains. This principle, first identified by Daniel Kahneman and Amos Tversky, reveals that the pain associated with losing is disproportionately greater than the pleasure derived from winning. In everyday life, this can manifest in various ways, from our reluctance to sell losing stocks to our preference for insurance against potential losses. Understanding loss aversion helps illuminate the intricacies of human decision-making, shedding light on why we often make choices that prioritize safety and security over potential gains.

Graphical Representation:

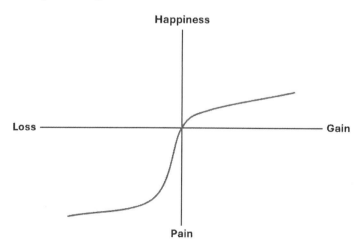

Graphical Key Points:

- The Gain part of the curve goes up, which means we feel happier as we gain more, but each extra bit we gain makes us a little less happy than the one before.
- The Losses part of the curve goes down, which means we feel more pain as we lose more. Again, each extra bit we lose adds less pain than the one before.
- The 'Loss' line drops more sharply than the 'Gain' line rises, highlighting a stronger reaction to losing something compared to the pleasure of gaining the exact same thing.

Life Scenario:

You find $50 on the street, which brightens your day slightly. Later, you lose $50 from your pocket. The annoyance of losing the money is much sharper than the pleasure you felt when you found the same amount. This highlights how losing money feels more impactful than the joy of finding money, even when the amount is exactly the same.

Wider Implications:

- **Investment Strategies:** In finance, understanding loss aversion can help investors make more balanced decisions, as it explains why some may hold onto losing stocks for too long or sell winning stocks too quickly.
- **Urban Planning:** Loss aversion can inform urban planning decisions, such as preserving historical buildings or green spaces, as communities often place a high value on avoiding the loss of these cherished assets.
- **Business Implications:** Loss aversion can influence decision-making in areas such as pricing strategies,

product development, and risk management. Companies often leverage this bias by emphasizing the potential losses customers might incur by not using their products or services, thereby encouraging purchase behavior.

Principle Origins:

Loss Aversion is a principle central to prospect theory, developed by Daniel Kahneman and Amos Tversky and introduced in their seminal paper, "Prospect Theory: An Analysis of Decision under Risk," published in 1979. In their research, they conducted various experiments and observed how people value potential losses and gains. In one of their experiments, they presented people with scenarios where they could choose between a certain loss and a gamble with a larger potential loss but also a chance to avoid losing anything. Despite the equal expected value, many chose the certain loss, illustrating their aversion to the larger potential loss. In another experiment, participants were told they could lose $10 if a coin landed on tails, but they could win a certain amount if it landed on heads. People generally didn't want to play this game unless the win was more than $20, showing they were more afraid of losing $10 than they were interested in the chance to win $20. This experiment from the late 1970s was crucial in demonstrating quantitatively that the discomfort associated with losing is more powerful than the pleasure of gaining.

Analyzing the Principle:

- **Losses Hit Our Survival Instinct:** Our brains are wired to prioritize survival. Losing resources feels like a threat to our well-being, so we react more strongly to prevent loss than to gain something extra.

- **Neuroeconomic Perspective:** Brain imaging studies in the field of neuroeconomics have shown that different regions of the brain are activated during the processing of gains and losses. The amygdala, in particular, is more active during loss-related decisions, suggesting a neurological basis for loss aversion.
- **Temporal Discounting:** Loss aversion interacts with the concept of temporal discounting, where individuals value immediate rewards more highly than future ones. This can lead to short-term decision-making that prioritizes avoiding immediate losses, even at the expense of long-term gains.

Insights to Implement in Life:

- **Reframe Losses as Opportunities:** When facing a potential loss, try to reframe it as an opportunity for learning or growth. For example, if you're hesitant to decide because you fear losing money, consider what you might gain in experience or knowledge, even if the financial outcome isn't favorable.
- **Diversify Your Options:** To minimize the impact of loss aversion on your decisions, consider diversifying your options. For example, when investing, spreading your assets across different types of investments can reduce the pain of loss in any one area and lead to more rational decision-making.
- **Practice Mindful Decision-Making:** Before making a decision, take a moment to assess whether your choice is being driven by the fear of loss. Mindfulness can help you recognize this bias and ensure that your decisions are based on a balanced evaluation of the situation.

Summary:

Loss aversion is a psychological bias that leads us to fear losses more than we value gains, significantly influencing our decision-making processes. By understanding and recognizing this bias, we can take steps to mitigate its impact and make more balanced and rational decisions in our everyday lives, allowing our motivation to be guided not by the fear of defeat, but by the desire for achievement.

Chapter 4: The Lindy Effect

"Time is the best judge of all things, what endures is what truly matters."

Principle Introduction:

The Lindy Effect serves as an early introduction to the power of simplicity in graphical representation. Not all graphs in this book are meant to be complex. Some, like the one illustrating this effect, are linear yet convey profound insights.

The Lindy Effect is a fascinating concept that suggests that the future life expectancy of certain non-perishable entities, such as ideas or technologies, is proportional to their current age. This principle, which finds relevance across various fields, offers a unique perspective on longevity and persistence.

Graphical Representation:

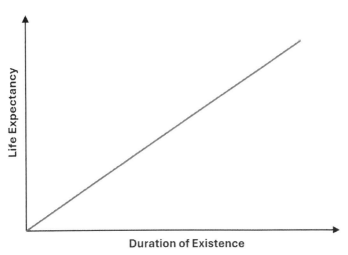

Graphical Key Points:

- **Emergence:** When something new is created, there's no history to predict its longevity.
- **Growth and Establishment:** This increase depicts the core idea of the Lindy effect – the longer some non-perishable entities have been in existence, the longer their expected remaining lifespan becomes. As an entity survives and gains years of operation, its projected future longevity increases proportionally.
- The Lindy effect can be observed in various domains, such as companies, restaurants, personal relationships, artistic works, academic theories, and more.

Life Scenario:

Technologies such as bicycles, the QWERTY keyboard layout, and analog watches, despite newer alternatives, continue to persist due to widespread adoption and integration into societal practices. This persistence illustrates the Lindy Effect beyond the realm of entertainment into practical and technological domains. Bicycles, for instance, remain a reliable mode of transportation over a century after their invention. The QWERTY keyboard layout, designed to prevent typewriter jams, is still widely used despite more efficient alternatives. Similarly, analog watches continue to be popular for their timeless design and reliability, maintaining their relevance as both functional timepieces and fashion accessories.

Wider Implications:

- **Business Forecasting:** The Lindy Effect offers a unique perspective in forecasting, allowing analysts to weigh

the longevity of businesses or stocks based on their past. Historically, companies that adapt and overcome various economic cycles may signal enduring success. However, this isn't a standalone tool, analysts combine it with other financial indicators to predict a company's future viability, ensuring a more rounded and robust forecast.
- **Social Circle:** New friends might come and go – their future in your life is not yet certain. Childhood friends, having weathered various life stages with you, tend to have a more assured place in your life – they've stood the test of time. Family and lifelong friends are the epitome of the Lindy Effect – the more years they've been in your life, the more likely they will continue to be, demonstrating a deep-rooted staying power in the social fabric of your existence.
- **Educational Content:** Educational techniques enduring the test of time often signal effectiveness, and the Lindy Effect supports this view. It posits that educational methods with a long-standing history in classrooms may continue to benefit learners. This principle encourages educators to respect the longevity of certain pedagogies while also emphasizing the need for continuous innovation and validation in the face of new educational research and societal changes.

Principle Origins:

The Lindy Effect was not derived from formal experiments but emerged from a combination of observational humor and later mathematical interpretation. It was first informally theorized at Lindy's deli in New York City by comedians who noticed a pattern regarding the longevity of a comedian's career based on their exposure. Albert Goldman formalized this observation in his "Lindy's Law" article for "The New Republic" in 1964. Benoit Mandelbrot provided a mathematical perspective in "The Fractal Geometry of Nature" in 1982, positing a relationship between the current age of non-perishables and their life expectancy. Nassim Nicholas Taleb then expanded on this in "The Black Swan" in 2007 and "Antifragile" in 2012, illustrating that objects or concepts that do not inherently degrade over time actually increase their chances of continued existence the longer they survive.

Analyzing the Principle:

- **Adaptation and Evolution:** Entities that survive over long periods often do so by adapting to changes in their environment. This continuous adaptation can make them more resilient to future changes. In the world of business, for instance, a company that has been around for a century has likely navigated multiple economic downturns, changes in consumer behavior, and technological disruptions, each time learning and evolving, thereby increasing its chances of survival.
- **Mistaking Age for Quality:** There's a common misconception that if something has been around for a long time, it must be superior. This isn't always the case. Some ideas, technologies, or products endure not because they are the best available options but due to factors like consumer habits, cost of change, or cultural heritage. For instance, QWERTY keyboards were designed to prevent typewriter jams in the past, not for typing efficiency, yet they are still widely used today despite the development of more efficient layouts.

- **Conditioned longevity:** It's essential to understand that the Lindy Effect is an observed principle that applies under specific conditions. It does not imply that something will continue to exist indefinitely simply because it has existed for a long time. There must be ongoing relevance and utility for continued existence. For example, ancient medical practices that have been around for thousands of years are sometimes considered effective merely due to their age, but many have been replaced by modern medicine for being outdated or disproven.

Insights to Implement in Life:

- **Filter the Hypes:** In a world brimming with fleeting trends, especially in technology, health, and lifestyle, the Lindy Effect can be your mental sieve. Before diving headfirst into the latest craze, pause and ponder: Will this trend endure the test of time, or is it just a passing phase? Opting for traditional choices might offer more lasting benefits. This approach helps you concentrate on aspects that genuinely enhance your life in the long run.
- **Embrace Time-Honored Relationships:** The Lindy Effect extends beyond mere objects or ideas; it also applies to relationships. Friendships and partnerships that have weathered various life stages are likely to be more resilient and rewarding. Invest time and effort in nurturing these enduring bonds, as they are likely to provide stability, support, and richness to your life for years to come.
- **Valuing Cultural Heritage:** The Lindy Effect posits that long-standing cultural works, like classic

literature, traditional music, and ancient art, will likely remain valuable. For example, the band Queen, which debuted in the 1970s, is expected to outlast many modern artists who may soon be forgotten. By valuing these timeless treasures, you not only deepen your own cultural understanding but also contribute to their preservation for future appreciation.

Summary:

The Lindy Effect is a thought-provoking concept that challenges us to view the world through the lens of longevity and resilience. It urges us to consider the wisdom embedded in practices and ideas that have stood the test of time, blending the allure of innovation with the rich insights of tradition. This perspective not only enriches our understanding of the present but also guides us in making choices that hold enduring value for the future.

Chapter 5: The Imposter Syndrome Interactive Chapter 1

"Are you even good enough to have the Imposter Syndrome?"

Graphical Representation:

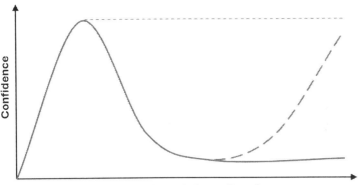

Actual Knowledge or Experience

Short Reminder:

In the end of each part, we'll dive into an interactive chapter that corresponds to a concept related to one of the previous chapters within that section. These interactive chapters are shorter than the regular chapters and tailored for you to reflect on and complete within your own mind. In this case, we will examine the imposter Syndrome and see how it contradicts the Dunning-Kruger Effect, which was introduced in the opening first chapter.

Principle Introduction:

The Imposter Syndrome is characterized by feelings of self-doubt and a fear of being exposed as a fraud, despite evidence of success. This syndrome can significantly impact the Dunning-Kruger Effect, where individuals with high skills are capable of accurately recognizing their high ability. However, due to the presence of Imposter Syndrome, they may paradoxically experience unwarranted low confidence in their abilities.

Ask Yourself:

- Do you notice these effects in others around you?
- How can recognizing the Imposter Syndrome and the Dunning-Kruger Effect enhance your perspective on life?
- How will you approach situations where you experience these feelings in the future?

Closing Thought:

As we unveil the complexities of the human psyche, it's important to recognize that feelings of inadequacy are common, even among the most successful individuals. Embracing our vulnerabilities and acknowledging our achievements can help us navigate the imposter syndrome and lead a more authentic life.

Part 2
The Fundamental Graphs

"Simplicity is the ultimate sophistication."

– Leonardo da Vinci

Welcome to the heart of our journey, where we explore the fundamental graphs that are the building blocks of life's principles. These graphs are not just abstract concepts, they are the lenses through which we can view and understand the world around us. As we dive into each graph, you'll start to see the connections between different areas of life, and how these principles are woven into the fabric of our everyday experiences.

Chapter 6: The Pareto's Law (The 80/20 Principle)

"Majority of the effect comes from the minority of the cause."

Principle Introduction:

Pareto's Law, also known as the 80/20 Principle, suggests that about 80% of outcomes come from just 20% of causes. This universal phenomenon applies across various fields, from business – where 80% of profits often come from 20% of customers, to personal productivity – where 20% of your efforts can yield 80% of your results. By identifying and focusing on this critical 20%, you can significantly boost your efficiency and effectiveness. This principle encourages a shift in perspective, urging individuals and organizations to prioritize their efforts on the most impactful areas, leading to a more optimized allocation of time, energy, and resources.

Graphical Representation:

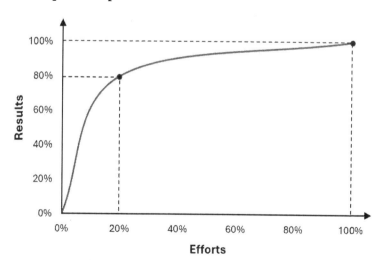

Graphical Key Points:

- The curve shows a steep rise at the beginning, indicating that the initial 20% of efforts yield an 80% impact.
- After reaching around 20% of effort, further efforts contribute less to the results.
- You can relabel the X-axis as "Contributors" or "Actions," "Factors," "Investment," and the Y-axis as "Outcomes" or "Results," "Rewards," "Gains" in order to exemplify Pareto's Law on the graph.

Life Scenario:

Most people wear 20% of their clothes 80% of the time. This means that out of all the clothes you own, you probably have a few favorites that you wear over and over again, while the rest sit in your closet most of the time.

Wider Implications:

- **Personal Finance:** In budgeting and spending, you might find that 80% of your expenses come from 20% of your purchases. By identifying and managing these key expenses, you can significantly improve your financial health.
- **Work and Productivity:** In a work setting, 20% of your tasks or projects might contribute to 80% of your achievements or results. Focusing on these high-impact tasks can significantly boost your productivity and career growth.
- **Health and Fitness:** In a fitness routine, 20% of the exercises or activities might contribute to 80% of your fitness results. Focusing on these effective exercises can optimize your workout efficiency.

Principle Origins:

Vilfredo Pareto, an Italian economist, first observed this principle in the early 20th century when he noticed that 80% of Italy's land was owned by 20% of the population. Further investigations revealed that this distribution was not only true in economics but also in various other realms. Pareto's initial observation has been extensively studied and validated in numerous fields since its inception.

Analyzing the Principle:

- **Efficiency Variance:** Naturally, not all inputs (resources, efforts, etc.) contribute equally to the output. Therefore, some inputs are inherently more productive and efficient. This results in an uneven distribution of output, where a few inputs can generate a disproportionate amount of the total output compared to the rest.
- **Systemic Preferences and Feedback:** Systems, such as markets or organizations, often reinforce the success of certain inputs, amplifying their effect in a self-reinforcing cycle. This is similar to the Rosenthal and the Matthew Effect, which you'll encounter later in the book, where higher expectations lead to better performance, showcasing how initial advantages can be magnified within a system.
- **Limitations and Misapplications:** The principle is more of a guideline than a strict rule. For example, in business, focusing solely on the 20% of products that generate 80% of the revenue can lead to neglecting emerging products or markets that could be crucial for future growth. This misapplication can result in overlooking important but less obvious factors.

Insights to Implement in Life:

- **Identify Your 20%:** Regularly analyze activities, customers, or products to identify the 20% contributing to most of your results, and redirect resources and efforts to maximize the impact of those key contributors.
- **Simplify Your Life:** Utilize the 80/20 rule to identify and eliminate the less impactful 80% of your belongings, commitments, investments, and activities. By focusing on the essentials, you can enjoy greater clarity and freedom in your daily life.
- **Apply It Across All Areas:** The Pareto Law can be applied across various fields such as business, personal development, health, education, time management, environmental conservation, marketing, and many more. Dedicate a specific time period to try and implement the law in each area of your life to enhance efficiency and effectiveness.

Summary:

The Pareto's Law suggests a universal truth about the imbalance of inputs and outputs. Understanding and applying this principle can lead to more efficient resource allocation in various aspects of life.

If you have really understood this law, you might realize that you're likely to remember only 20% of the book's chapters well, and inevitably, slowly forget the rest (no offense intended – it's simply how our brains operate). That 20%? It's your goldmine of everyday insights. The rest? It's like the spare change in your wallet – not always in immediate use, but invaluable when needed.

Having said that, be careful of overgeneralization – sometimes, you need to use the Pareto's Law as a guiding principle rather than a strict rule, staying open to nuances and exceptions. Who knows? Maybe you'll remember all 52 chapters in the book.

Chapter 7: The Law of Diminishing Returns

"After a certain point, the more you have, the less you get."

Principle Introduction:

The Law of Diminishing Returns, a cornerstone of economic theory, demonstrates that beyond a certain point, additional investments in production yield smaller increases in output, and eventually, the total output may even decrease. This principle highlights the limits of efficiency and the importance of balancing resources for sustainable growth.

Graphical Representation:

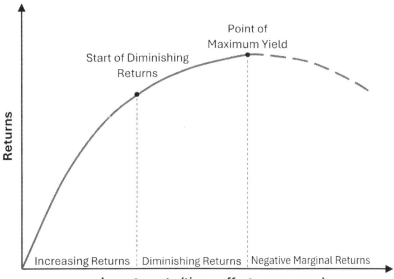

Graphical Key Points:

- **"Rise of Productivity"** – The initial climb where each new input significantly boosts productivity.
- **"Optimal Efficiency Level"** – The point where output per unit of input is maximized.
- **"Beyond the Peak"** – The inefficiency that may occur when investments exceed the optimal level.

Life Scenario:

Imagine a student preparing for an exam. Initially, each additional hour spent studying significantly improves their understanding and retention of the material. However, after several hours, the student becomes tired, and each additional hour of studying leads to smaller increases in their understanding. Eventually, studying too much can lead to lack of sleep, exhaustion, and decreased performance. This scenario illustrates how beyond a certain point, additional study time leads to diminishing returns in terms of learning and exam performance.

Wider Implications:

- **Fitness:** In the initial workouts, changes are most significant – muscle gains and improvements in strength occur rapidly. However, over time, these benefits diminish, making further progress harder to achieve.
- **Marginal Utility:** The first slice of pizza provides the most satisfaction, but each additional slice offers less. Similarly, $1,000 is more valuable to a poor man than to a wealthy man. This reflects Marginal Utility, the added satisfaction a consumer gets from each additional unit of a good or service, which decreases over time.

- **Group Dynamics and the Flow State (Chapter 2):** When more and more people participate in the same complicated task, the challenge for each individual can decrease, potentially leading each one to the boredom zone, as depicted in the Flow State chapter. This reduction in individual engagement and enjoyment can sometimes be so significant that overall production may eventually decrease.

Principle Origins:

The Law of Diminishing Returns was first articulated by economists such as Anne Robert Jacques Turgot, Johann Heinrich von Thünen, and David Ricardo in the 18th and 19th centuries. It was not based on a single experiment and emerged from observations of farming productivity. David Ricardo illustrated the principle using the example of land cultivation. He observed that as more labor and capital were applied to a fixed amount of land, the additional yield from each successive unit of input began to decline. This observation led to the formulation of the Law of Diminishing Returns, highlighting the importance of optimal resource allocation in maximizing productivity and economic efficiency.

Analyzing the Principle:

- **Initial Use of Best Resources:** Initially, the most efficient and productive resources are utilized. As production expands, less efficient or lower-quality resources are employed, leading to a decrease in the additional output produced per unit of input.
- **Output Limitation:** Every output has a limit. As you increase inputs and outputs, you approach the maximum

level of returns you can produce. Once you reach this limit, you can no longer enjoy the benefits of increased energy. It's similar to continuing to advertise when you are unable to manufacture additional products.
- **Increased Complexity in Investments:** As production scales go up, the costs of coordinating and managing the logistics and processes of the increased amount of inputs may rise faster than production gains, resulting in inefficiencies of large scale.

Insights to Implement in Life:

- **Strategic Retreat from Overindulgence:** Retreat before excess takes its cost. Knowing when to pull back on investment, be it time, money, or resources, can be the shield against the arrows of diminishing fortunes.
- **Delayed Retreat:** Sometimes, missing the exact point of optimal retreat isn't catastrophic. The initial phase beyond the peak often shows only a slight decrease in output. The key is to monitor closely and adjust before the decline becomes steep.
- **Balance Work and Pleasure:** Apply the concept of diminishing returns to your work-life balance. Working excessively long hours can lead to decreased productivity and overall well-being. Find the sweet spot where your work yields maximum results without compromising your health or personal life.

Summary:

Incorporating the Law of Diminishing Returns into our lives can be transformative. It teaches us to set realistic goals, find a healthy work-life balance, and make smart investments. This principle serves as a reminder that sometimes, less can be more.

Speaking of which, I could have tried to write 152 chapters instead of only 52, but in the spirit of this law, I chose less. After all, adding more chapters might have diluted the impact, leading to less engagement for you and potential burnout for me. So, in a way, you're welcome!

Chapter 8: Compound Interest

"Compound interest is the eighth wonder of the world. He who understands it, earns it. He who doesn't, pays it."

– Albert Einstein

Principle Introduction:

Compound interest, often hailed as one of the most powerful forces in finance, is equally potent when applied to the realm of personal development. It illustrates how small, regular investments in skills or habits can accumulate and multiply over time, leading to significant growth and improvement.

Graphical Representation:

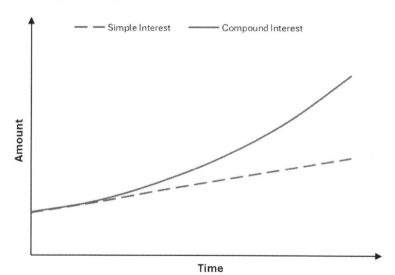

Graphical Key Points:

- **Simple Interest:** The dashed line representing simple interest shows a steady, straight-line increase over time. Simple interest means you earn the same amount of interest every period on the initial amount you invested.
  For example, you invest $100 in a bank for 50 years with a 5.00% fixed interest rate per year:
  - After the first year, you will have plus 5% of $100 = $105.
  - After the second year, you will have plus 5% of $100= 110$.
  - After the third year, you will have plus 5% of $100 = $115.
  - After 50 years, you will have a total of $350.
- **Compound Interest:** The solid line representing compound interest curves upwards, growing faster as time goes on. Compound interest means you earn interest not only on your initial amount but also on the total amount earned in the previous period. For example, you invest 100$ in a bank for 50 years with a 5.00% compounded interest rate per year:
  - After the first year, you will have plus 5% of 100$ = 105%.
  - After the second year, you will have plus 5% of 105$ = 110.25%.
  - After the third year, you will have plus 5% of 110.25$ = 115.76$.
  - After 50 years, you will have a total of 1,146.74$.
- **Comparison:** As time passes, the gap between the compound interest and simple interest lines widens,

showing that the amount of money you can earn with compound interest increases much more over time.

Life Scenario:

Compound interest isn't just a financial principle, it's also a powerful tool for personal growth. For example, in learning a new language, one approach focuses on continuously revisiting and integrating previous lessons, effectively compounding knowledge over time. This method, similar to how compound interest works, significantly enhances retention and understanding. In contrast, studying new material without integrating past lessons, akin to simple interest, results in a linear and potentially slower acquisition of knowledge.

Wider Implications:

- **Relationship Building:** Underlining the importance of consistent, small efforts in nurturing relationships, where each positive interaction and shared experience builds upon the last, leading to deeper and more meaningful connections over time.
- **Skill Acquisition:** Highlighting the gradual accumulation of knowledge and skills through consistent practice, where each learning session builds on the previous ones, leading to exponential growth in proficiency.
- **Health and Fitness:** Stressing the long-term advantages of maintaining a consistent exercise and nutrition regimen, where small, daily health choices can lead to significant improvements in overall well-being over time.

Principle Origins:

The concept of compound interest, with its roots in ancient Babylon, was documented in Balducci Pegolotti's 14th-century Italian book 'Pratica della mercatura,' which translates to 'The Practice of Commerce.' The book provided insights into the trade and commerce practices of the time. The mathematical foundations of compound interest were further developed in the 17th century, notably by Richard Witt in his 1613 work "Arithmetical Questions." This book, dedicated entirely to the subject, contained comprehensive tables and practical examples of compound interest calculations, formalizing its understanding. Jacob Bernoulli's discovery of the constant e in the late 17th century marked a significant milestone in the mathematical development of compound interest. Unlike simple interest, which generates a constant return, compound interest accumulates wealth as interest earns interest over time, becoming a fundamental financial concept in modern economics and finance.

Analyzing the Principle:

- **The Power of Consistency:** One of the key factors in the effectiveness of compound interest is consistency. The more consistently you invest or apply effort, the stronger the momentum becomes. This is because each period of interest or growth builds upon the previous one, creating an accelerating effect. Just like a snowball rolling down a hill, the more consistently you keep pushing, the bigger and faster it grows.
- **The Power of Early Beginnings:** The longer you allow your investment or effort to compound, the

more substantial the results. This is why starting early, even with small contributions, can lead to impressive outcomes over the long term.
- **Frequency of Compounding:** The frequency with which interest is compounded also affects the growth of an investment. Compounding more often, like daily instead of monthly, leads to faster growth compared to annual compounding.

Insights to Implement in Life:

- **Start early, even if it seems small:** The earlier you start, the more you benefit from the compounding effect. Even small beginnings can lead to significant outcomes over time. Begin with what you can, whether it's saving a small amount of money each month, dedicating only 10 minutes a day to learning a new skill, or taking a short 5-minute walk every morning.
- **Stay consistent, build momentum, cultivate patience:** Regular contributions ensure continuous growth, with each addition building on the previous ones. Make these contributions a fixed part of your routine to maintain the momentum. Remember that Compound Interest also requires time to work its magic, with the most significant growth in the later years of an investment.
- **Compound Interest vs. The Law of Diminishing Returns:** The contradiction between compound interest and the law of diminishing returns (Chapter 7) lies in balancing patience with vigilance. Embrace the power of compound interest by investing patiently for exponential growth. At the same time, stay alert to the law of diminishing returns, recognizing when

further investments yield diminishing rewards. This balance between persistence and timely action is the key to maximizing your returns and making wise decisions in life.

Summary:

Compound interest serves as a powerful analogy for the principle that consistent, small efforts can lead to substantial growth over time. Whether in finance, skill-building, or personal habits, the principle reinforces the value of patience, consistency, and the strategic use of time for exponential gains.

Chapter 9: Cognitive Dissonance

"It's a shame cars don't run on cognitive dissonance."

– Lewis Black

Principle Introduction:

Cognitive dissonance theory helps us understand why we sometimes feel uncomfortable when what we think and what we do don't match up. For instance, if you value healthy eating but indulge in an entire pizza, you're likely to feel a sense of discomfort. This sensation is cognitive dissonance, it's like your brain is saying: "Hey, something's not right here." To get rid of this discomfort, you might change what you believe (convince yourself that pizza isn't so bad) or change how you act (decide to eat healthier next time). This theory is important because it shows how much we like things to make sense in our heads and how we'll change our thoughts or actions to make sure they do.

Graphical Representation:

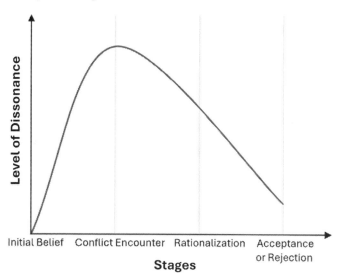

Graphical Key Points:

- **Initial Belief:** Comfortable with existing beliefs, no dissonance. Example: valuing healthy eating.
- **Conflict Encounter:** Dissonance spikes when encountering contradictory information/behavior. Example: Eating an entire pizza.
- **Rationalization:** This stage involves finding the best reasons to minimize the inconsistency between the beliefs and actions, but the dissonance is still present, albeit at a lower level compared to the Conflict Encounter stage. Example: "I deserved this pizza after a tough day" or "I'll compensate by eating healthier tomorrow."
- **Acceptance or Rejection:** Dissonance is greatly reduced when the individual either modifies their beliefs to align with the new information or behavior or rejects the conflicting information. Example: "Occasional indulgences are okay as long as I maintain a generally healthy lifestyle," or "Pizza is actually healthier than people actually think."
- The progression through cognitive dissonance stages can be swift and can take less than 10 seconds, evidencing the mind's nimble reconciliation of discordant cognitions.

Life Scenario:

A voter who supports a political candidate may experience dissonance if the candidate's actions contradict their values, leading them to change their support or justify the candidate's behavior.

Wider Implications:

- **Marketing:** Companies may use cognitive dissonance to their advantage by highlighting the benefits of a product to make consumers feel good about their purchase, even if it's expensive.
- **Investment Decisions:** An investor holds onto losing stocks, convincing themselves they'll rebound, rather than admitting the loss.
- **Gambling:** Players might lose repeatedly but continue playing, convinced their luck will turn or that they're improving. Justifications like: "My luck will turn" and "I'm learning and getting better" aren't rational.

Principle origins:

The foundational study that introduced the principle of cognitive dissonance was conducted by Leon Festinger and his colleagues in 1956. They infiltrated a UFO cult that expected a flood to end the world but believed they'd be saved by a spaceship. The researchers observed the cult's reactions when the predicted apocalypse did not happen. The cult members coped with the disconfirmation by rationalizing that their actions had prevented the disaster, thus maintaining their belief system and self-esteem. This observation led to Festinger's formulation of cognitive dissonance theory, which posits that people experience discomfort when their beliefs are challenged, leading them to change their beliefs or adopt new ones to reduce dissonance. This study showed how far individuals would go to preserve their beliefs and avoid admitting they were wrong and the discomfort of cognitive dissonance.

Analyzing the Principle:

- **Seeking Consistency:** Our brain operates with harmony. When what we do clashes with what we believe, it feels off. This is like trying to listen to a song when the notes don't match – it just doesn't sound right. Cognitive dissonance happens because we're trying to get the melody of our beliefs and actions to match up again.
- **Changing Beliefs Over Admitting Mistakes:** It's easier for us to change our story than to admit we're wrong. For example, when the cult's prophecy didn't come true, they couldn't accept their mistake. Instead, they changed their belief to fit the outcome. It's like if you miss a shot in basketball and instead of saying you missed, you claim you were passing it.
- **Group Influence:** Being part of a group can strengthen the process. The cult members had friends who shared their beliefs, so they stuck to their guns even harder to avoid being the odd one out. It's similar to cheering for a sports team – even if they lose, you find reasons to support them because your friends do.

Insights to Implement in Life:

- **Question Your Justifications:** When you find yourself rationalizing a decision that doesn't feel right, pause, and reassess. Are you justifying it to avoid discomfort, or does it genuinely align with your values? By questioning your justifications, you can make more authentic choices.
- **Balance Adaptation:** Recognize that while cognitive dissonance can push you to adapt quickly, it's essential to find a balance. A strong mindset involves

knowing when to adjust to the true reality and when to confront challenging information. Don't rush to resolve dissonance at the expense of your values or well-being. Instead, take the time to evaluate what's genuinely best for you in the long run.
- **Challenge Your Comfort Zone:** When you feel uneasy about trying something new, remind yourself that growth usually comes after passing the discomfort from the cognitive dissonance. Embrace these opportunities to expand your horizons and use your cognitive dissonance recognition as a motivator to step out of your comfort zone.

Summary:

Cognitive dissonance is a powerful psychological phenomenon that drives individuals to seek consistency between their beliefs and actions. Understanding and managing dissonance is essential for personal development, effective decision-making, and successful interpersonal relationships.

Chapter 10: Emotional Cycle of Change

"Change is hard at first, messy in the middle and gorgeous at the end."

– Robin Sharma

Principle Introduction:

The Emotional Cycle of Change is a conceptual roadmap of the psychological stages experienced during the process of intentional change. Developed by psychologists Don Kelley and Daryl Conner in the mid-1970s, this model elucidates the emotional highs and lows that accompany personal or organizational transformations. Interestingly, the Emotional Cycle of Change bears a resemblance to the Dunning-Kruger Effect by highlighting a journey of awareness and understanding. However, while the Dunning-Kruger Effect focuses on the paradox of our own ignorance, the Emotional Cycle of Change emphasizes the emotional journey encountered during the learning and change process.

Graphical Representation:

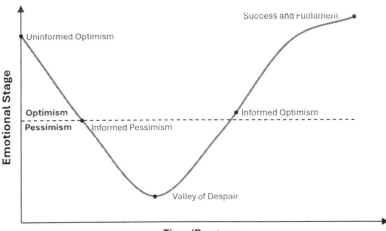

Graphical Key Points:

- **Uninformed Optimism:** This represents the initial excitement and high expectations when starting a new endeavor, usually without a full understanding of the challenges ahead.
- **Informed Pessimism:** As individuals progress and face obstacles, they gain a more realistic understanding of the challenges involved, leading to a decline in optimism and potential feelings of frustration or discouragement.
- **Valley of Despair:** This is the lowest emotional point, where individuals face the hardest challenges and the temptation to quit is strongest. It's a test of resilience and commitment.
- **Informed Optimism:** After surviving the valley, this point marks the phase of renewed confidence, where lessons learned from previous hardships lead to a more realistic and strategic approach to achieving the goal, setting the stage for eventual success and fulfillment.
- **Success and Fulfillment:** The final stage, where individuals achieve their desired outcome, having navigated the emotional ups and downs of the change process. They feel a sense of accomplishment and satisfaction, having grown and learned from the experience.

Life Scenario:

You move into a new apartment, excited about the new space and opportunities (Uninformed Optimism). Soon, you discover issues like noisy neighbors or plumbing problems (Informed Pessimism). Feeling frustrated and questioning your choice (Valley of Despair), you take steps to address these issues. Gradually, you adapt and find solutions, growing more comfortable and confident in your new home (Informed Optimism). Eventually, your apartment becomes a personal haven (Success & Fulfillment).

Wider Implications:

- **Entrepreneurship and Start-ups:** Entrepreneurs and start-up founders often experience the Emotional Cycle of Change as they navigate the highs and lows of launching and growing a new business, from the initial excitement and optimism to the challenges and setbacks that can lead to the Valley of Despair.
- **Athletic Training and Performance:** Athletes and coaches can use the Emotional Cycle of Change to understand and manage the emotional aspects of training and competition, from the initial enthusiasm and optimism to the challenges and self-doubt that can arise during tough training periods or after setbacks.
- **Education:** Teachers and students can utilize this model to manage emotions during the learning process, particularly when dealing with complex subjects or skills.

Principle Origins:

Don Kelley and Daryl Conner developed their Emotional Cycle of Change model in the mid-1970s and outlined it in their Handbook for Group Facilitators. The model captures the emotional highs and lows that individuals experience during intentional change, whether personal or organizational.

Analyzing the Principle:

- **Rose-Tinted Beginnings:** Every new journey, from trying a new restaurant to starting a new relationship often starts with rose-tinted glasses, where optimism blinds us and sets the trap of unrealistic expectations that can heighten future frustration.
- **Psychological Resilience:** The transition from the Valley of Despair to Informed Optimism is crucial and relies heavily on psychological resilience. This shift involves reframing setbacks as learning opportunities and modifying one's emotional response to challenges. It's a testament to one's ability to adapt thoughts and behaviors in response to adversity.
- **The Connection to Cognitive Dissonance:** The Emotional Cycle of Change intersects with Cognitive Dissonance (Chapter 9) during stages like Informed Pessimism and the Valley of Despair. Dissonance arises when reality clashes with initial expectations, causing psychological discomfort. Addressing this dissonance is crucial for progressing to Informed Optimism and achieving successful change outcomes.

Insights to Implement in Life:

- **Lower your Expectations Before You Start:** Intentionally setting lower expectations early in the change process can help soften the emotional impact of the Valley of Despair.
- **The Valley of Despair is Inevitable:** Recognize that the Valley of Despair is an inevitable part of the change process. Preparing for this phase by planning coping strategies and support mechanisms can transform a potentially overwhelming experience into a manage-

able one. This foreknowledge empowers you to persevere through the toughest times with a clear vision of the path forward.
- **Value Each Stage as Progress:** No matter which stage you are in, recognize that every step, even the setbacks, contributes to your overall progress. Valleys of Despair can be lengthy and could occur several times, but they are still a crucial part of the journey.

Summary:

The Emotional Cycle of Change offers a profound insight into the flow of our emotional state during times of transition. It serves as a beacon, guiding individuals and organizations through the turbulent waters of change, from uninformed optimism to the rewarding shores of success and fulfillment.

Chapter 11: The Forgetting Curve

"Memory is the treasury and guardian of all things."

– Marcus Tullius Cicero

Principle Introduction:

The Forgetting Curve, conceptualized by Hermann Ebbinghaus, is a pivotal model in understanding memory erosion over time. It suggests that memory retention decreases exponentially over time without active efforts to retain information. This principle has profound implications for educational strategies, personal development, and understanding human cognition.

Graphical Representation:

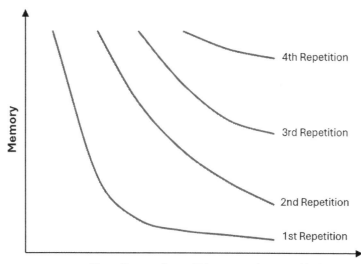

Graphical Key Points:

- **Memory Peak:** The graph shows that at the start of each repetition, memory retention is at its highest.
- **Memory Declines over Time:** Memory retention naturally declines over time if nothing is done.
- **Each Repetition Slows the Rate of Forgetting:** With each subsequent repetition, the decline in memory retention becomes less steep and we get longer retention of the same information.

Life Scenario:

Imagine you've moved to France for work and started to learn French. After an initial burst of intensive learning, work demands pull you away from practice, and soon, basic conversations become a struggle. By maintaining regular reviews using apps, attending meetups, and revisiting notes, you counteract memory loss, demonstrating the power of frequent repetition in mastering new skills.

Wider Implications:

- **Fitness Routines:** Repeating exercises helps muscle memory, ensuring that movements become more automatic and less easily forgotten.
- **Academic Success:** Frequent review of material and summarizing key concepts after study sessions improve memory retention and recall during exams.
- **Music Learning:** Regularly practicing and playing musical pieces can solidify music skills, combating the forgetting curve.

Principle Origins:

The forgetting curve was first proposed by Hermann Ebbinghaus in 1885, he conducted experiments on himself using made-up words like "wid," "zof," and "qax" to study memory and forgetting. Ebbinghaus found that memory retention declines rapidly after learning, with most forgetting occurring within the first hour. He plotted these results in a graph, now known as the forgetting curve, which shows an exponential decrease in memory retention over time.

Analyzing the Principle:

- **Memory Fades Naturally:** Our brains are built to let go of information we don't use. Like clearing out old files on a computer, it's a way to keep our minds uncluttered.
- **Repetition is Key:** Reviewing information multiple times helps strengthen the connections in your brain, similar to how exercising a muscle makes it stronger. Each time you practice recalling a fact or concept, it becomes more firmly embedded in your long-term memory, making it easier to remember in the future.
- **Variability in Memory Retention:** The Forgetting Curve varies across individuals, it's influenced by the emotional significance and personal relevance of information, as well as the complexity of the subject matter. Emotionally charged or personally significant material often leads to stronger and more enduring memories, altering the typical pattern of forgetting. Simultaneously, complex information may be more challenging to retain and could steepen the initial decline in memory retention.

Insights to Implement in Life:

- **Repeat to Enhance Your Baseline Memory Retention:** It's essential to establish a routine where you regularly revisit the material you're learning at fixed intervals, dedicating a set amount of time to each session. This consistent repetition helps strengthen the connections in your brain related to the learned content, making it easier to recall in the future.
- **The Opposite of Forgetting is Writing:** Don't overestimate your memory ability, it's often not as reliable as you might think. Instead, make a habit of writing things down. Whether it's taking notes during a meeting, maintaining a daily journal, or using a planner to track tasks and appointments, writing serves as a backup for your memory and aids in organizing and prioritizing your thoughts and responsibilities.
- **Prioritize Sleep on Memorizing:** Not getting enough sleep can significantly accelerate the rate of forgetting, aim to get 7-9 hours of sleep each night and establish a consistent sleep schedule. By prioritizing sleep, you can slow down the rate of forgetting and enhance your overall memory retention.

Summary:

In this chapter, we explored Hermann Ebbinghaus's groundbreaking model, which illustrates how our memories are as fleeting as a politician's promises during election season. This principle, with its roots in the 19th century, not only survived the test of time but also shed light on why cramming the night before an exam often leads to forgetting faster than you can say "Ebbinghaus." The graphical representation shows us that memory is like a leaky bucket – without constant refilling (or repetition), what we've learned gradually escapes us.

Here's a tip and a gentle nudge: If you're starting to forget what the previous chapters of this book covered, don't worry, it's just your brain doing some spring cleaning. Consider this your cue to engage in a bit of mental decluttering. Flip back through the pages, give those earlier concepts another look, and remind yourself of the insights you've gathered. Think of it as a mini workout for your brain, keeping those memory muscles flexed and ready. After all, you wouldn't want to forget the laws and principles that can elevate your daily life, would you?

Chapter 12: The Gaussian Distribution

"Nature's great book is written in mathematics."

– Galileo Galilei

Principle Introduction:

The Gaussian Distribution, often referred to as the Normal Distribution, is a fundamental concept in statistics representing the idealized distribution of values around a mean. Its all-over presence across natural and social sciences makes it a cornerstone for understanding variability in complex systems.

Graphical Representation:

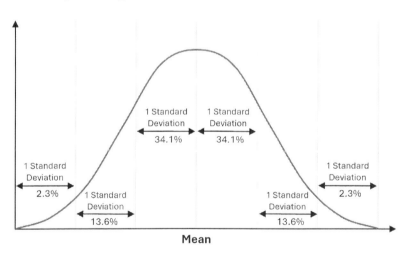

Graphical Key Points:

- **Peak at the Mean:** The highest point of the curve is at the mean value. This indicates where most of the data points are.

- **Symmetrical Distribution:** The graph shows a symmetrical, bell-shaped curve centered around the mean. This indicates that data points are equally distributed around it, with the majority of the values clustering near the center of the distribution.
- **Standard Deviation:** The curve is segmented into sections that represent standard deviations from the mean. In this example, one standard deviation to the left and right of the mean includes 34.1% of the data each, two standard deviations include 13.6% each, and three standard deviations include only 2.3% each. This demonstrates how data points are spread out and that most of the data (about 68.2%) lies within only one standard deviation from the mean.

Life Scenario:

Consider a school where the analysis of test results is common practice. Most of these results hover near the median, with some outstandingly high or low exceptions. Such a spread of results generally takes the shape of a Gaussian curve, reflecting the typical range of performance variance.

Wider Implications:

- **Market Research:** Understanding consumer behavior patterns, such as purchase frequency and preferences.
- **Genetic Trait Distribution:** Biologists use Gaussian distributions to study variations in genetic traits across populations, aiding in understanding evolutionary patterns and health predispositions.
- **Environmental Policy:** Used in modeling climate change scenarios, predicting temperature and sea-level changes over time.

Principle Origins:

The Gaussian Distribution, also known as the Normal Distribution, was developed by Carl Friedrich Gauss, a brilliant German mathematician. Gauss, in the early 19th century, was analyzing astronomical data and needed a way to handle measurement errors. He developed this distribution as a method to describe the error in his measurements, showing how often each error size occurred. The bell-shaped curve, later termed the Gaussian Distribution, became a foundational concept in statistics, representing how various phenomena naturally cluster around an average value.

Analyzing the Principle:

- **Central Limit Theorem Connection:** The Gaussian distribution is closely linked to the Central Limit Theorem. This theorem states that when you add up a large number of random variables from any distribution with a defined mean and variance, their sum tends towards a Gaussian distribution.
- **Ubiquity in Nature:** The Gaussian distribution appears in various natural phenomena, from people's height and blood pressure readings to rainfall amounts and the distribution of test scores. It even shapes the patterns of errors in measurements and stock market fluctuations.
- **Misinterpretation Risks:** While useful, the Gaussian model can be misleading when applied to data with significant outliers or non-standard distributions.

Insights to Implement in Life:

- **Stand Out in Daily Routines:** To excel above average, add a unique twist to everyday activities. For example, wearing a more sophisticated outfit than expected for an event can set you apart. By personalizing your approach, you distinguish yourself from the masses, ensuring you're not just another face in the crowd, but a memorable presence beyond the average.

- **Average Often Wins:** Most values in a Gaussian distribution are close to the mean, making the average a stable and predictable point. In many contexts, such as manufacturing or service performance, being close to the average can mean consistency and reliability, which are highly valued in producing quality products and delivering dependable services.
- **Clarifying the Misunderstanding of Feedback's Impact on Performance:** When someone performs exceptionally well at a certain task and at the following attempt their performance drops, or if they perform poorly and subsequently improve, it's common to credit these shifts largely to the feedback they received after the first attempt: Positive feedback might boost their motivation, while negative feedback could make them approach the task with greater diligence. However, what's usually occurring is a phenomenon known as regression toward the mean, where performance naturally returns to its average level. This phenomenon indicates that both exceptionally good and exceptionally poor performances tend to stabilize over time due to a variety of factors, not just feedback. By assuming that feedback alone is responsible for these changes, we overlook other crucial influences like natural variability and other random factors. When evaluating your own performance or the performance of others, it's essential to maintain a balanced perspective. While feedback is a valuable tool for growth and improve-

ment, it's crucial not to overestimate its impact or attribute changes in performance solely to the feedback received.

Summary:

The Gaussian Distribution is a powerful tool for understanding the spread and central tendency of data in various fields. Its bell-shaped curve is a fundamental image in statistics, illustrating how data tends to cluster around a mean, and providing a baseline for measuring deviation and understanding variability.

Chapter 13: Stigler's Law of Eponymy

"Everything of importance has been said before by somebody who did not discover it."

— Alfred North Whitehead

Principle Introduction:

Stigler's Law of Eponymy, humorously named by Stephen Stigler himself, states that no scientific discovery is named after its original discoverer. This phenomenon reflects the complex nature of credit and recognition in the scientific community and beyond.

Graphical Representation:

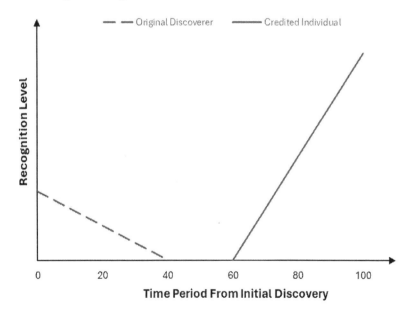

Graphical Key Points:

- The graph shows two intersecting lines: one for the original discoverer and one for the credited individual.
- The recognition level of the original discoverer decreases over time, as shown by the dashed line descending.
- In contrast, the recognition level of the credited individual starts afterward and increases over time, indicated by the solid line ascending.

Life Scenario:

Gaussian Distribution is a great example. While named after Carl Friedrich Gauss, who significantly contributed to its mathematical development, the initial concept can be traced back to Abraham de Moivre. In his 1738 work "The Doctrine of Chances," de Moivre introduced an approximation to the binomial distribution, which laid the groundwork for the normal distribution.

Wider Implications:

- **Legal Patents:** The allocation of credit and patents can sometimes reflect Stigler's Law, where the first to file, not the first to invent, is recognized.
- **Media and Journalism:** How stories and breakthroughs are attributed to the most visible or vocal individuals, rather than the original sources.
- **In academia:** Recognition of the contributions of lesser-known researchers.

Principle Origins:

Stigler's Law of Eponymy was articulated by the statistician Stephen Stigler in his 1980 publication "Stigler's Law of Eponymy." In this work, Stigler humorously named the law after himself, even though he acknowledged that the concept could be traced back to earlier thinkers. He credited the sociologist Robert K. Merton with the idea, citing Merton's work on the sociology of science, which explored how scientific discoveries are often named after individuals who are not their original discoverers. It is important to note that the effect described by Stigler's Law may be cyclical and not a one-time occurrence, as subsequent generations might continue to attribute discoveries to more recent or prominent figures, further obscuring the true originators.

Analyzing the Principle:

- **The Value of Publication and Marketing:** Priority of discovery is often tied to the first good publication of the idea. This emphasis on publication can lead to misattributions when the original discoverers do not publish their work promptly.
- **Winners Write History:** The prominence of historical figures is often shaped by the cultural, political, or social context of their times. For instance, Christopher Columbus is widely celebrated as the original discoverer of America in 1492, overlooking Norse explorer Leif Erikson, who, according to earlier proofs, reached the continent almost 500 years earlier. This disparity in recognition stems from the significant impact and extensive documentation of Columbus's voyages during a peak period of European exploration and colonization, which aligned with narratives of European superiority.

- **The Matthew Effect:** The Matthew Effect (Chapter 16) is the idea that those who are already successful, tend to receive more recognition and resources compared to their less successful ones, even when their achievements are similar. Stigler's Law shows this in action, as famous individuals are frequently credited for discoveries instead of the lesser-known real discoverers, reinforcing the Matthew Effect.

Insights to Implement in Life:

- **Operate with the Assumption of Competition:** Assume that someone else in the world has already thought of your new startup or invention idea. Let this assumption fuel your motivation to move quickly in developing and executing your idea before anyone else does. Acting with this mindset prevents complacency and laziness, driving you to take decisive action and stay ahead of potential competitors.
- **Claim Your Credit:** Actively speak up about your contributions in meetings, reports, or emails. Don't wait for others to notice, make sure your work is seen and acknowledged. By being direct about your achievements, you prevent them from being overlooked or forgotten.
- **Embrace Humility in Success:** Stigler's Law reminds us that many achievements are built on the contributions of those who came before us. In your personal and professional life, recognize and acknowledge the collective efforts that have paved the way for your successes. This humility fosters a collaborative spirit and keeps you grounded, reminding you that every accomplishment is part of a larger tapestry of human endeavor.

Summary:

Should I be wary of someone stealing my book's idea and putting their name on it in the future?

Is there at least one quote at the beginning of each chapter that I haven't properly attributed to the original speaker?

I should be careful; this law is tricky.

Chapter 14: The Baader-Meinhof Phenomenon Interactive Chapter 2

"Once you notice something, it's everywhere."

Graphical Representation:

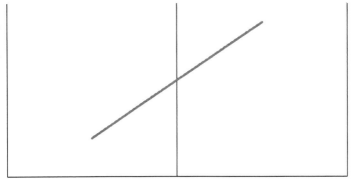

Perceived Frequency of Encountering New Information

Principle introduction:

The Baader-Meinhof Phenomenon, also known as frequency illusion, is a fascinating cognitive bias that involves the experience of suddenly noticing a concept, word, or thing everywhere shortly after learning about it. This phenomenon can make it seem like new information is appearing with improbable frequency, though it's simply a result of increased awareness. Understanding this phenomenon offers insights into how our brains process and filter information, influencing our perceptions of the world around us.

Reflective Exercise:

Reflect on the graph depicting how awareness amplifies our perception of frequency. Ask yourself:
- When was the last time you experienced this phenomenon? Was it a word, an idea, a song?
- How did this heightened awareness influence your interactions or decisions in the following days or weeks?
- Imagine other concepts or objects that might currently be in your blind spot. How could shifting your awareness bring new frequencies into focus?

Closing Thought:

As we progress through the book, each new chapter brings forth a fresh law/effect/idea that we may not have recognized before. Then, suddenly, we start seeing it everywhere! It's important to realize that this effect, too, is a hidden phenomenon of life.

Part 3
The Social and Organizational Graphs

"Culture eats strategy for breakfast."

– Peter Drucker

Step into the world of social and organizational graphs, where we unravel the complexities of human interaction in society, business, and education. This part is all about understanding the relationships that shape our world, from personal bonds to professional networks. As we navigate through these graphs, you'll gain insights into the underlying forces that drive our connections and collaborations. Get ready to explore the intricate dance of human interaction and discover how these social structures influence our lives in profound ways.

Chapter 15: The Rosenthal Effect (Pygmalion Effect)

"Expectations are the seeds of greatness."

Principle Introduction:

The Rosenthal Effect, or Pygmalion Effect, explores how high expectations can lead to improved performance. Named after psychologist Robert Rosenthal, it addresses the impact of belief and expectation on people's abilities and outcomes.

Graphical Representation:

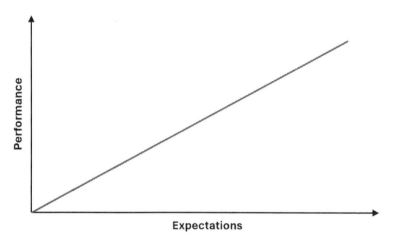

Graphical Key Points:

- **Starting Point:** When expectations are low, performance tends to be low.

- **High Expectations lead to high Performance:** As seen in the graph's end, high expectations correlate with high performance levels.
- The line moves steadily upward without any ups and downs. However, in real-life scenarios, variations are common, and we might expect to see fluctuations in performance as expectations change.

Life Scenario:

Imagine a manager who believes that one of their team members has the potential to excel in leadership roles. The manager expects high performance and often entrusts this employee with challenging projects and provides them with constructive feedback and encouragement. Motivated by their manager's high expectations and support, the employee works harder, sharpens his skills, and eventually progresses into a leadership position, exceeding his own and others' initial expectations for his performance.

Wider Implications:

- **Parenting:** Parents should express confidence in their children's abilities and maintain high expectations. This can encourage children to develop a strong belief in their capabilities, leading to better effort and achievement.
- **Team Dynamics:** Teams that collectively hold high expectations for their performance tend to collaborate more effectively, innovate, and overcome challenges, leading to superior team results.
- **Athletic Rehabilitation:** A professional athlete recovering from an injury typically experiences a faster and

more effective recovery process than average athletes when both their physiotherapist and they themselves set high recovery expectations.

Principle Origins:

The Rosenthal Effect originates from a 1968 study by psychologist Robert Rosenthal and school principal Lenore Jacobson. They informed teachers that certain students were potential "intellectual bloomers" based on a fictitious test. These randomly selected students showed significant academic improvement, demonstrating that teacher expectations could greatly influence student performance. This study highlighted the impact of self-fulfilling prophecies in educational and other settings.

Analyzing the Principle:

- **Initial Belief:** The impact of low expectations can initiate a detrimental cycle, similar to how high expectations can foster positive outcomes. For example, when a teacher has low expectations from a student's abilities, this can translate into less supportive and less engaging interactions. If the teacher believes the student cannot handle complex math problems, they may refrain from assigning such tasks, effectively limiting the student's opportunity to learn and grow.
- **Behavioral Confirmation:** The student, sensing the lack of support and challenging opportunities, may start to doubt his own abilities. This can lead to a decrease in effort and engagement, as he feels it's not expected of him to perform well.
- **Reinforcing Cycle:** The student's lowered performance confirms the teacher's initial low expecta-

tions, which further diminishes the teacher's efforts to engage the student. This creates a negative cycle where the student's potential is consistently undermined.

Insights to Implement in Life:

- **Set High Expectations for Others:** Whether you're a manager, teacher, or mentor, setting high expectations can naturally lead to improved performance in your team or students. People often rise to meet the expectations set for them, so aiming high can encourage them to maximize their potential.
- **Caution with Consequences of Low Expectations:** Reassess in your life with whom you have a negative expectations cycle. Provide supportive reinforcements regardless of your high or low expectations. When people know that they are doing a good job and that their efforts are recognized, they are more likely to continue to work hard and improve. Constructive feedback should also be encouraging and focused on how to continue to develop skills and competencies.
- **Challenge Yourself with High Goals:** Create challenging goals for yourself that stretch your abilities. Check in on your progress often and remind yourself that you have the capability to meet these high standards. This self-focused approach uses the Pygmalion effect to boost your own growth and performance.

Summary:

The Rosenthal Effect highlights the significant influence of expectations on performance outcomes. While understanding and leveraging this principle can lead to enhanced performance in various domains of life, it's important to acknowledge the potential negative impact of low expectations. Low expectations can inadvertently limit individuals, stifling their potential and hindering their ability to excel. Thus, maintaining high expectations, both for oneself and for others, is essential for unlocking untapped potential and achieving optimal results. Striving to cultivate a positive and supportive environment that encourages growth and success is key to navigating the dual nature of the Rosenthal Effect.

Chapter 16: The Matthew Effect

"Early advantage begets later advantage."

Principle Introduction:

The Matthew Effect, a term coined by sociologist Robert K. Merton, describes the phenomenon where "the rich get richer and the poor get poorer" in various contexts, including but not limited to economics, education, and science. This principle illustrates how initial advantages lead to further gains while initial disadvantages hinder progress.

Graphical Representation:

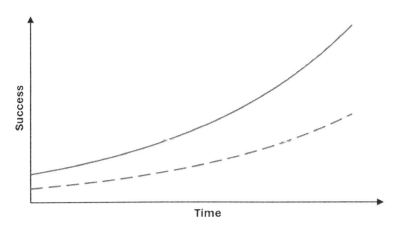

Graphical Key Points:

- **Initial Advantage:** Depict how small initial differences in advantage can start.
- **Growth Over Time:** Show an exponential growth in both lines.

- **Comparative Stagnation:** Despite the same growth factor, the gap increases as time passes.

Life Scenario:

One child grows up in a home rich with educational resources and receives additional tutoring, gaining a significant head start in school. This early advantage leads to more attention from teachers and access to advanced opportunities, resulting in scholarships and a path to higher education. Another child, equally capable, starts with fewer resources and struggles to catch up due to less personalized support. This illustrates the Matthew effect in education: the first child's initial lead compounds into greater success, while the second child's early disadvantage makes achieving similar outcomes much more challenging.

Wider Implications:

- **Music Industry:** Well-known musicians or bands have an advantage in getting their new songs on popular playlists or radio stations compared to emerging artists. Their existing fan base and industry connections help amplify their new releases, leading to more widespread recognition and success.
- **Job Market:** Individuals with strong professional networks or prestigious internships early in their careers may find it easier to secure desirable job offers compared to those without such advantages. This initial success can then lead to a more accelerated career trajectory.
- **Film Industry:** Established actors or directors are more likely to secure funding and distribution for their

new projects compared to newcomers. Their track record of successful films and industry relationships make them more appealing to investors and studios, resulting in greater exposure and box office success for their new films.

Principle Origins:

The origin of the "Matthew effect" traces back to the seminal work of sociologist Robert K. Merton in 1968, where he introduced the term to describe the phenomenon in which well-established scientists receive disproportionately more recognition and credit for their contributions than lesser-known researchers, despite similar levels of achievement. Merton drew the term from a passage in the Gospel of Matthew in the Bible, encapsulating the idea that: "To everyone who has, more will be given, but from the one who has not, even what he has will be taken away." His analysis focused on the social structures within the scientific community that facilitate this unequal distribution of recognition, highlighting how such dynamics not only affect individual careers but also shape the broader landscape of scientific research and knowledge production. The Matthew Effect has since been applied broadly across disciplines, highlighting systemic inequalities.

Analyzing the Principle:

- **Resource Accumulation:** Individuals who start with an advantage, whether it be in terms of wealth, knowledge, or social connections, are often in a better position to accumulate additional resources. Sometimes, this initial advantage is justified due to previous achievements, but not always. This advantage enables them to access opportunities that further their growth, such as better education, networking opportunities, or investment returns, which in turn leads to even greater advantages over those who start with less.

- **The Rosenthal Effect (Chapter 15):** The Matthew Effect and the Rosenthal effect (Pygmalion Effect) intersect in their demonstration of expectancy's power. Just as teachers' expectations of students' success can significantly impact their performance, societal expectations based on initial success or failure can amplify future outcomes. Both effects underscore the self-fulfilling prophecy of expectations in determining individual success or failure.
- **Compound Interest (Chapter 8):** The Matthew Effect also connects beautifully to the principle of Compound Interest, emphasizing the importance of the initial conditions. Similar to compound interest, where a higher starting amount leads to faster growth, the Matthew Effect suggests that an initial advantage can accelerate success faster.

Insights to Implement in Life:

- **Early Advantage Matters:** Recognize the importance of early advantages and strive to provide them to those who may not have enough. This could include early education, mentorship, or access to resources that can set individuals on a positive trajectory.
- **Starting Behind, Winning Ahead:** Initial advantages don't always determine future success. Sometimes, the person with less at the beginning but more potential can surpass others who had a head start. It's important to assess everyone's capabilities accurately before

diving in. For example, in basketball, a tall player who can't aim is less effective than a shorter player with excellent aim.
- **Equity-Based Approaches:** Implement policies and practices that consciously counteract the Matthew Effect by redistributing resources to reduce initial disparities.

Summary:

The Matthew Effect encapsulates the principle of cumulative advantage, highlighting the importance of initial conditions in determining long-term outcomes. By connecting this chapter to previous chapters, we can see how the concept of cumulative advantage has been built upon and expanded. Understanding and addressing the mechanisms through which advantages are compounded can help us work towards a more equitable and balanced society.

Chapter 17: The Peter Principle

"In an organization, each person rises to the level of his own incompetence."

– Laurence J. Peter

Principle Introduction:

As a company CEO, choosing between promoting an outstanding or mediocre technician employee for a managerial vacancy is more complex than you think. Common sense might lead you to choose the superior performer, but this could be a mistake according to the Peter Principle. The principle suggests that employees are often promoted based on their current performance until they reach a position where they are no longer competent. Consequently, organizations risk becoming populated with employees unfit for their managing roles, which is detrimental in the long run.

Graphical Representation:

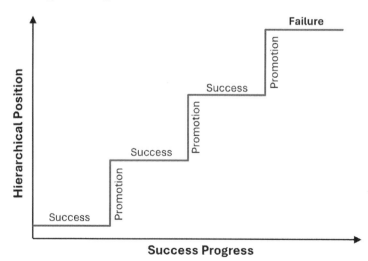

Graphical Key Points:

- An individual's success in a current position leads to a promotion.
- With each promotion, the individual ascends higher in the organizational hierarchy.
- Eventually, a promotion may result in the individual reaching a position where they fail, reflecting the Peter Principle's concept of rising to one's "level of incompetence."

Life Scenario:

A standout teacher excels in the classroom and is then promoted to principal, a role demanding different skills like budgeting and strategic planning. If these skills are not in the teacher's repertoire, their promotion leads to a plateau of productivity and effectiveness, an example of the Peter Principle at work.

Wider Implications:

- **Software Developer to Project Manager:** A software developer who excels at coding and problem-solving is promoted to project manager. They may find it difficult to manage timelines, coordinate with different teams, and handle client communication, as their strengths are in technical development rather than project management.
- **Sports Team:** A top-performing athlete might be promoted to a coaching position where strategic planning and team management are key, areas that may not align with their athletic talents.
- **Military:** A decorated soldier, professional in tactical operations, may rise to a command position that

demands strategic oversight – a skill set that extends beyond frontline engagement, potentially stretching their capabilities.

Principle Origins:

The Peter Principle was introduced by Dr. Laurence J. Peter in his 1969 book "The Peter Principle: Why Things Always Go Wrong," co-authored with Raymond Hull, as a result of Dr. Peter's observations on organizational behavior. The principle was presented humorously through anecdotes and fictional examples, rather than being based on formal experiments or empirical research. Despite this, it has sparked debate and research in management and organizational psychology, with some studies attempting to empirically test its implications. The principle's enduring popularity lies in its ability to capture a common workplace experience, making it a classic in discussions about career progression and organizational effectiveness. In 2018, almost 50 years after its initial publication – the Peter Principle has been scientifically confirmed.

Analyzing the Principle:

- **Different Roles Require Different Skills:** The fundamental issue in organizations is the tendency to promote employees based on their achievements in their current roles. While this might seem logical, it often overlooks the fact that different roles require different skills. As a result, individuals who excel in one position might not necessarily perform well in a higher role with different demands.

- **Rewarding Top Performers:** There's a natural inclination for managers to reward their best performers with promotions as a means of keeping them motivated and satisfied. However, this can lead to situations where the new role isn't well-suited to the employee's skill set, even though they deserved the promotion for their past performance.
- **Inadequate Evaluation Processes:** Without proper evaluation, employees may be promoted based on factors like seniority or popularity, rather than their ability to perform in the new position. Additionally, there may not be a robust system in place to prevent the promotion of long-tenured employees with poor performance.

Insights to Implement in Life:

- **Adaptability in Career and Life Transitions:** The Peter Principle emphasizes the need for adaptability and recognizing that past success doesn't ensure future effectiveness. It's essential to continuously learn and acquire new skills to succeed in different environments. This notion also reminds us to be mindful of the Dunning-Kruger effect (Chapter 1) when embarking on new roles, cautioning against overestimating our abilities in unfamiliar territories.
- **Strive for Skills Alignment:** Before pursuing a promotion or new opportunity, assess whether the role aligns with your skills, interests and career aspirations. Ensure that you have a clear understanding of the responsibilities and expectations of the new position and evaluate how well they match your strengths and areas for growth. This alignment can lead to greater

job satisfaction and can even save you from 'The Anxiety Zone' (The Flow State – Chapter 2).
- **Work on Your Managing Skills:** In addition to technical skills, focus on developing your managing skills and emotional intelligence (EQ), which includes self-awareness, self-regulation, empathy, and social skills. High EQ can enhance your ability to lead, communicate, and collaborate effectively, making you better equipped to handle the challenges of higher-level roles.

Summary:

The Peter Principle is a thought-provoking concept that challenges the traditional approach to promotions within hierarchical organizations. It underscores the critical need for organizations to assess the distinct skills required for each role and to implement robust evaluation processes for promotions. So, don't be surprised next time you see your boss struggle with their responsibilities. It could be a classic case of the Peter Principle in action, revealing the limitations of conventional promotion practices.

Chapter 18: The Milgram Obedience Experiment

"Ordinary people, simply doing their jobs, and without any particular hostility on their part, can become agents in a terrible destructive process."

– Stanley Milgram

Principle Introduction:

This chapter delves into the psychological underpinnings of obedience, as revealed by the Milgram Experiment. It discusses how the experiment's outcomes shed light on the complex interplay between authority, conformity, and individual moral judgment.

Graphical Representation:

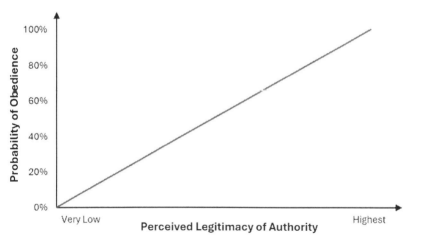

Graphical Key Points:

- **Rise in Obedience:** As the perceived legitimacy of authority increases, so does obedience, even for actions that are not legitimate.
- **Near-Total Obedience:** When an authority is perceived as highly legitimate, individuals may largely set aside their own moral judgment, potentially reaching a near-absolute level of obedience.
- **Starting Point and Angle of the Graph:** More legitime action or a more obedient person results in a higher starting point and steeper ascent.

Life Scenario:

In military settings, soldiers often follow orders from their commanding officers without question, even in high-stress combat situations. This obedience to authority is crucial for maintaining discipline and coordination in the armed forces but can also lead to controversial actions when soldiers carry out orders that may conflict with their personal morals or international laws, such as in the case of wartime atrocities.

Wider Implications:

- **Law Enforcement:** Understanding compliance in interactions between police and civilians.
- **Politics:** How political leaders' perceived legitimacy affects public compliance with policies.
- **Family Dynamics:** Parental authority and children's obedience patterns.

Principle Origins:

The Milgram experiment, conducted by psychologist Stanley Milgram in the 1960s, was a series of social psychology experiments that measured the willingness of participants to obey an authority figure who instructed them to perform acts conflicting with their personal conscience. In the most famous variant, participants were led to believe they were administering electric shocks to a "learner" (an actor) for incorrect answers in a memory test. Despite the learner's feigned screams and pleas for mercy, a significant majority of participants continued to administer shocks when prompted by the experimenter, demonstrating the powerful influence of authority on obedience. The experiment revealed the unsettling capacity for ordinary individuals to commit harmful actions when directed by an authority figure, highlighting the potential dangers of blind obedience and the importance of ethical conduct and personal responsibility. This insight into human behavior was particularly relevant in understanding actions during the Holocaust.

Analyzing the Principle:

- **Authority and Fear of Consequences:** Humans' innate respect for societal hierarchies and authority figures often compels obedience, even against personal morals. This obedience is further reinforced by the fear of negative repercussions, like punishment or social ostracism for defiance. These intertwined aspects underscore the complex dynamics between authority adherence and the fear of facing consequences,

emphasizing how deeply societal norms and the anticipation of penalties can influence individual actions.
- **Diffusion of Responsibility:** In the presence of an authority figure, individuals may feel less personally responsible for their actions, believing that the responsibility lies with the one giving the orders. This diffusion of responsibility can reduce the cognitive dissonance (Chapter 9) associated with performing unethical actions, making it easier for individuals to comply.
- **Conformity and Group Dynamics:** The desire to fit in and be accepted by a group can influence individuals to follow the actions of an authority figure, especially when others are also complying. This social pressure can lead to conformity, even when it means going against one's own values or ethical standards.

Insights to Implement in Life:

- **Cultivate Critical Thinking:** Encourage the development of critical thinking skills to evaluate situations and authority figures objectively. This means questioning directives, understanding the rationale behind decisions, and considering the ethical implications of actions. By fostering a mindset that values inquiry and skepticism, you can make more informed choices and resist undue influence.
- **Establish Personal Boundaries:** Set clear personal boundaries that define what is acceptable and what is not in terms of obedience to authority. This involves identifying core values and principles and being prepared to assertively communicate and uphold these boundaries when faced with pressure to conform. By

knowing and respecting one's limits, you can navigate authority dynamics while maintaining personal integrity.
- **Nurture Personal Accountability:** Take ownership of your choices and actions, regardless of the influence of authority figures. Develop a strong sense of personal accountability by regularly reflecting on the consequences of your decisions and their impact on others. This mindset empowers you to make conscious choices aligned with your values, rather than blindly following orders or rationalization of unethical behavior.

Summary:

The Milgram Experiment exposes to us the chilling capacity for authority to compel unquestioning obedience. This renowned study delves into the darker realms of human behavior, revealing how intense external pressures can enable true cruelty to manifest. The experiment underscores the urgent need for moral courage and critical thinking to prevent unleashing our harmful potential when blindly following authority.

Chapter 19: The Bystander Effect

"In the end, we will remember not the words of our enemies, but the silence of our friends."

– Martin Luther King Jr.

Principle Introduction:

The Bystander Effect is a psychological phenomenon where individuals are less likely to offer help to a victim when other people are present. This counterintuitive behavior is rooted in the diffusion of responsibility, where the presence of others leads each person to feel less personally responsible for taking action. The Bystander Effect highlights the complex interplay between individual psychology and group dynamics, shedding light on how social context influences moral decisions.

Graphical Representation:

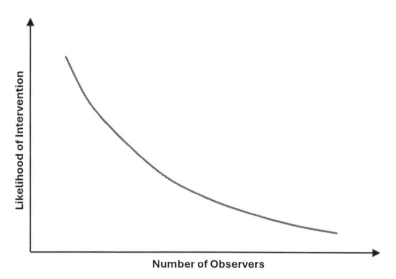

Graphical Key Points:

- At the start, with only a few observers, the intervention is most probable.
- The graph immediately shows a steep decline, illustrating how the likelihood of someone helping drops as the number of bystanders increases.
- At the end the curve almost flattens out, indicating that with many observers, the chance of anyone helping becomes quite low.

Life Scenario:

In a busy park, a child is lost and crying. Most assume that someone else will attend to the child, this collective inaction delays the child's much-needed assistance.

Wider Implications:

- **Emergency Situations:** Understanding this effect can improve emergency response strategies in public places.
- **Bullying Prevention:** In educational programs, emphasizing individual responsibility can motivate students to act against bullying, rather than assuming others will intervene.
- **Workplace Harassment:** Promote a culture of zero tolerance for harassment, urging employees to report incidents immediately rather than assuming someone else will address the issue.

Principle Origins:

The murder of Kitty Genovese in 1964 is often cited as a key event leading to the formal investigation of the

Bystander Effect. Genovese was attacked and eventually murdered outside her apartment while multiple neighbors reportedly observed or heard the attack but failed to help or call the police. Initially, it was reported that 38 witnesses did nothing, fostering widespread public outrage. Later investigations showed evidence of fewer witnesses and some attempts to help, but the narrative had already spurred social psychologists Bibb Latané and John Darley to study the phenomenon scientifically. Their studies revealed that people were less likely to help a victim when other witnesses were present. Their research shed light on the psychological mechanisms behind this behavior, changing the way we understand social responsibility and group dynamics.

Analyzing the Principle:

- **Diffusion of Responsibility:** When more people are present, individuals feel less personal responsibility to act. This diffusion is a psychological defense, as people assume others will take charge, diluting their own sense of obligation.
- **Social Influence:** People in groups tend to monitor the reactions of others to determine if action is necessary. If no one else seems concerned, individuals interpret the situation as non-urgent.
- **Evaluation Apprehension:** Potential helpers may fear being judged by their actions, worrying about overreacting or embarrassing themselves if they misinterpret the situation.

Insights to Implement in Life:

- **Recognize and Act:** Develop an acute awareness of the bystander effect. In crowded settings, make a

deliberate effort to step forward and intervene when necessary.
- **Break the Silence:** Foster a culture of openness and proactive intervention. Encourage individuals to speak up and take action in scenarios where injustice or harm is observed, dismantling the barriers of silence.
- **Advance Role Assignment:** Assigning specific roles to individuals ahead of time can counteract the bystander effect in action. This forward-thinking strategy ensures that everyone knows their responsibilities before emergencies arise, leading to a faster and more coordinated response. This approach encourages bystanders to become proactive participants, both in urgent situations and in everyday contexts.

Summary:

The Bystander Effect is a powerful illustration of how social dynamics can influence individual behavior, often leading to inaction in critical situations. By understanding this phenomenon, we can work towards fostering a culture of responsibility and empathy, where individuals feel empowered to act, even in the presence of others.

Chapter 20: The Hawthorne Effect

"All eyes on you."

Principle Introduction:

The Hawthorne Effect reveals how individuals and animals alter their behavior in response to being observed. This chapter explores the profound implications of this effect on research methodologies, workplace productivity, and educational practices, highlighting the complex interplay between observation and human behavior.

Graphical Representation:

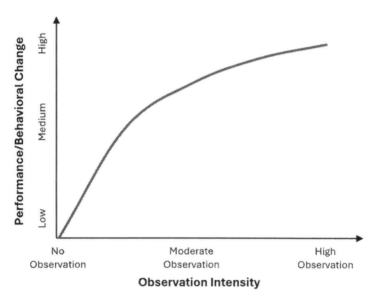

Graphical Key Points:

- When there is no observation or monitoring, individuals tend to exhibit no significant change in their performance or behavior compared to their typical patterns.
- With a moderate level of observation or awareness of being studied, individuals often demonstrate an elevated level of performance or a noticeable positive change in their behavior, surpassing their usual or average level.
- Under high levels of observation or intense scrutiny, individuals commonly experience a substantial boost in their performance or a significant positive adjustment in their behavior, reaching peak levels compared to their typical conduct.

Life Scenario:

Athletes often perform better under the watchful eyes of their coaches. The intensity of observation correlates with performance levels – the closer and more attentive the coach's observation, the better the athletes perform. Conversely, the moment a coach diverts their attention, there's a dip in the athletes' effort and output.

Wider Implications:

- **Organizational Behavior:** Designing work environments to leverage the positive aspects of the Hawthorne Effect (For example, installing cameras likely leads to an immediate increase in workers' performance).
- **Fitness Group Challenge:** A group of friends tracking their exercise and diet together on a shared platform is likely to see impressive initial results. But as the novelty

wore off and the sense of observation faded, their motivation and progress plateaued.
- **Pet Behavior:** Animals also show improved obedience and perform tricks more reliably when their owners are watching.

Principle Origins:

The origins of this effect can be traced back to the Hawthorne Works factory experiments conducted by Elton Mayo and his team in the 1920s and 1930s, which aimed to examine how different conditions affected workers' productivity. Unexpectedly, they found that almost any change in conditions or the mere act of being observed led to improved productivity, introducing the Hawthorne Effect into the lexicon of social and behavioral sciences.

Analyzing the Principle:

- **Self-Awareness:** When people are aware that they are being observed or monitored, they become more self-conscious about their actions. This heightened self-awareness leads them to alter their behavior in an attempt to present themselves in a more favorable light or conform to what they perceive as expected or desirable.
- **Psychological Visibility:** People perform better when they feel visible and acknowledged. The quality of being seen validates their work and existence, increasing engagement and effort.
- **Authority Influence:** Performance improvement is more significant when the observer is someone of authority or someone the individual greatly appreci-

ates. The desire to impress or not disappoint can motivate higher effort and focus.

Insights to Implement in Life:

- **Self-Monitoring:** Implement self-monitoring techniques, like journaling or habit-tracking apps, to simulate an observer effect, encouraging personal accountability and improvement.
- **Imagined Observation:** Trick yourself into performing better by imagining someone you respect or aim to impress is observing you. This mental practice can lead to improved decision-making and performance, mimicking the benefits of actual observation.
- **Constructive Visibility:** In leadership roles, actively observe and acknowledge your team's efforts. This visibility can enhance motivation and performance, leveraging the Hawthorne Effect positively.

Summary:

The Hawthorne Effect underscores the significant impact of observation on human behavior, offering valuable insights for improving workplace productivity, educational strategies, and research methodologies. By understanding and ethically applying this principle, we can foster environments that enhance performance and motivation through constructive observation.

Chapter 21: The Streisand Effect

"Don't think of a pink elephant."

Principle Introduction:

The Streisand Effect encapsulates the paradoxical phenomenon where attempts to hide, suppress, or censor information only amplify its public exposure. Named after a famous incident involving Barbara Streisand, this principle highlights the counterproductive outcomes of trying to control information and explores the dynamics of human curiosity, digital communication, and the often unpredictable consequences of trying to silence voices or information.

Graphical Representation:

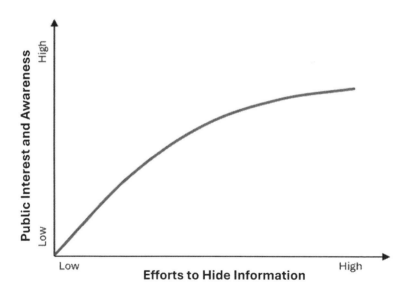

Graphical Key Points:

- **Direct Relationship from the Start:** When there are low efforts to hide information, public interest and awareness remain low.
- **Curve Shape:** As the efforts to restrict information grow higher, the public's attention to the information also grows higher.
- **Plateau:** The highest efforts to hide information correlate with the highest levels of public interest and awareness.

Life Scenario:

A mayor demands the removal of graffiti, criticizing city policy from public walls. The story is picked up by local news, and images of the graffiti spread across social media, leading to a city-wide debate about the very policy the mayor aimed to shield from scrutiny.

Wider Implications:

- **Personal Privacy:** An individual's attempt to remove embarrassing content online, only to see it go viral.
- **Government Censorship:** A government's effort to suppress a news article, resulting in increased international attention.
- **Crisis Communication:** Strategies for organizations to effectively address potentially damaging information.

Principle Origins:

The concept now known as the Streisand Effect was inadvertently introduced by Barbra Streisand in 2003, when she attempted to suppress an aerial photograph of her home. This backfired and led to widespread publicity, increasing the photograph's circulation. Mike Masnick officially coined the term "Streisand Effect" in 2005. It came about during a discussion of a different censorship attempt. This time, a beach resort issued a takedown notice to a website called urinal.net for featuring a photo of a urinal with the resort's name mentioned. This seemingly insignificant photo would have likely gone unnoticed, but drawing from the Streisand incident, Masnick speculated that trying to suppress online content usually results in that content getting more attention. His prediction was accurate, as efforts to hide the urinal photo only increased its visibility.

Analyzing the Principle:

- **Curiosity:** Just like the forbidden fruit, the more you tell someone they can't have something, the more they want it. This curiosity drives the spread of information.
- **Psychological Reactance:** People have a psychological response to regain freedom when they perceive it is being restricted. The Streisand Effect is often a mass-scale demonstration of this reactance.
- **Social Proof and Virality:** When something is suppressed, and yet everyone seems to be talking about it, it creates social proof, compelling even more people to share and discuss it.

Insights to Implement in Life:

- **Manage Mistakes with Humility:** When you attempt to cover up an error and it gets uncovered, it can harm your reputation more than the error itself. A better approach is to acknowledge mistakes with humility

and take responsibility. This is applicable in all walks of life, from handling accidents at work to personal relationships. By owning your mistakes and outlining steps to prevent future occurrences, you not only demonstrate integrity but also turn the situation into a learning opportunity for yourself and others.
- **Counter-Intuition in Problem-Solving:** When faced with a challenge, sometimes the most intuitive solution isn't the most effective. Like the Streisand Effect demonstrates, trying to suppress something can make it more visible. Apply this in daily life by considering counter-intuitive approaches when traditional methods fail. For instance, if you're struggling to overcome procrastination, instead of forcing yourself to work, take a short, mindful break. This can recharge your mental batteries and improve focus when you return to the task.
- **Streisand Effect for Marketing:** You can use the Streisand Effect as a strategic marketing tool by intentionally attempting to 'suppress' information about a product or service that you actually want to publicize. For instance, you can create a marketing campaign around a 'leaked' piece of information about a new product feature or an 'insider secret' that the company doesn't want the public to know. This can pique the public's interest and generate buzz.

Summary:

The Streisand Effect serves as a powerful reminder of the complex relationship between information control and public curiosity. In an era where information is freely accessible and easily shared, attempts to suppress often lead to greater visibility. This principle encourages a thoughtful approach to information management, emphasizing transparency and strategic communication over attempts at control.

Chapter 22: The Spotlight Effect

"You wouldn't worry so much about what others think of you if you realized how seldom they do."

– Eleanor Roosevelt

Principle Introduction:

The spotlight effect, also known as the illusion of transparency, refers to the tendency for people to overestimate the degree to which their own actions, appearance, or behaviors are noticed and evaluated by others. It's the feeling that a spotlight is shining on us, making our every move more noticeable than it actually is.

Graphical Representation:

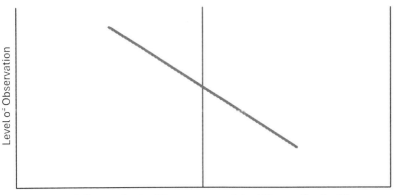

Graphical Key Points:

- The left part represents the 'Perceived Observation by Others,' showing that individuals often perceive

a high level of observation and scrutiny in various social situations.
- The right depicts the 'Actual Observation by Others,' which is significantly lower, indicating that in reality, people are observed or noticed much less than they think.
- This graph captures the disparity between perception and reality in the context of the Spotlight Effect, highlighting how we tend to overestimate the extent to which our actions and appearance are noticed by others.

Life Scenario:

At a party, you spill a drink and feel as if all eyes are on you. In reality, most guests are too engaged in their own conversations to notice.

Wider Implications:

- **Public Exercise:** Working out in public areas, such as parks or gyms, might make people feel as if they're being watched and judged, whereas others are typically preoccupied with their own exercise routines.
- **Virtual Meetings Self-View:** During virtual meetings on any platform with camera functionality, individuals often focus intensely on their own image, believing others are equally observant of them. However, most attendees are usually more concerned with how they appear themselves.
- **Public Performance:** The pressure performers feel under the gaze of an audience.

Principle Origins:

This cognitive bias was first identified and studied by researchers Thomas Gilovich, Victoria Husted Medvec, and Kenneth Savitsky in a series of experiments conducted in the late 1990s. One of the foundational studies that introduced the spotlight effect was published in 2000 in the Journal of Personality and Social Psychology, where they conducted experiments to investigate people's perceptions of how conspicuous their actions or appearance were to others. In one experiment, participants were asked to wear an embarrassing T-shirt while walking around a campus and estimate the percentage of people who had noticed it. The results showed participants consistently overestimated the degree to which others had noticed their T-shirt. In another experiment, participants took a quiz while wearing a Barry Manilow T-shirt and overestimated how many peers noticed it, compared to actual reports.

Analyzing the Principle:

- **Egocentric Bias:** The spotlight effect is closely tied to the egocentric bias, which is our tendency to view the world primarily from our own perspective and underestimate the perspectives of others. We often fail to consider that others may be preoccupied with their own thoughts, concerns, and experiences, rather than fixated on our every move or quirk. This difficulty in taking others' perspectives contributes to the overestimation of how much we are noticed or evaluated.
- **Emotions and Memory Distortion:** Emotionally salient or embarrassing experiences tend to be more vividly encoded in our memories, potentially leading to a distortion in how noticeable we perceive them to be. When we do something that elicits strong emotions, such as embarrassment or anxiety, those feelings can

amplify our perceptions of how much others noticed or evaluated the situation. Our memories of these emotional experiences may also become exaggerated over time, further reinforcing the spotlight effect.
- **Low Self-Confidence:** Low self-confidence can intensify the spotlight effect. When lacking confidence, individuals become more self-conscious and assume others are critically evaluating their perceived flaws. This heightened self-focus and fear of negative judgment amplifies the belief that one is the center of attention, overestimating how much others notice their actions or appearance. Higher self-confidence can help buffer against the distorted perceptions of the spotlight effect.

Insights to Implement in Life:

- **Remove the Obstacles to Action:** Overcome barriers that hinder your ability to take decisive action by understanding the deepness of the spotlight effect and reducing the weight you give to others' opinions. Identify the specific fears or doubts that hold you back, such as fear of judgment, failure, or rejection. Challenge these fears by questioning their validity and considering the worst-case scenarios.
- **Embrace Imperfection:** Recognize that perfection is an unattainable goal and that striving for it can lead to unnecessary stress and self-criticism. Instead, embrace imperfection by acknowledging your strengths and weaknesses, and focus on continuous improvement. This mindset can be applied in personal growth, relationships, and even in creative endeavors, where the beauty often lies in the uniqueness and authenticity of the imperfect.

- **Enhance Public Speaking and Performance:** If you're someone who experiences stage fright or performance anxiety, the spotlight effect might be intensifying these feelings. Before a presentation or performance, remind yourself that the audience is likely to be more forgiving and less focused on minor mistakes than you anticipate. Focus on the key messages you want to convey and remember that your audience is there to learn from you, not to judge every small detail. This acknowledgement can help you approach public speaking with more confidence and ease.

Summary:

The Spotlight Efect reminds us that we are often our own harshest critics, and that the world doesn't scrutinize our every move. Understanding this can liberate us from the chains of self-consciousness, allowing us to live more freely and authentically.

Did you notice I confidently misspelled "Effect"? Good for you! I personally don't care. It's because I know that even if you notice, you will forget it in the next 5 minutes. This is a great acknowledgement of the Spotlight Effect; I'm proud of myself.

Chapter 23: The Spotlight Effect Through Life's Stages
Interactive Chapter 3

"Care about people's approval, and you will always be their prisoner."

— Lao Tzu

Graphical Representation:

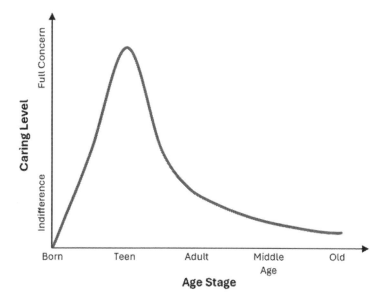

Reflective Exercise:

Examine the graph depicting the fluctuating levels of concern for others' opinions throughout life's stages. Reflect on your journey and compare to the added graph representation:

- How has the significance of others' perceptions changed for you over the years?
- At which life stage did you find yourself most influenced by others' views?
- Compare my graphical representation with the changes you perceive in your level of concern and caring level over the years.

Closing Thought:

Remember, your life is yours to live, people will always have something to say. Sometimes you need to accept criticism, but most of the time, you don't. Regardless, always stay true to yourself and your own path.

Part 4
The Decision-Making Graphs

"We are our choices."

– Jean-Paul Sartre

Welcome to the realm of decision-making graphs, where we delve deep into the art and science of making choices. In this part, we'll explore the cognitive biases and mental processes that shape our decisions, from the simplest daily choices to life's most complex dilemmas. As we uncover the mechanisms behind our thinking, you'll gain valuable insights into how to make more informed and effective decisions. Prepare to challenge your assumptions and refine your decision-making skills as we journey through the fascinating landscape of human thought.

Chapter 24: The Sunk Cost Fallacy

"The only real battle in life is between hanging on and letting go."

– Shannon L. Alder

Principle Introduction:

The Sunk Cost Fallacy reflects our tendency to continue a course of action or relationship due to past investments of emotion, time, or energy, despite current dissatisfaction or harm. This is largely driven by the fear of wasted effort, where individuals continue with a decision to avoid feeling like their initial effort was in vain. However, other interesting factors also contribute to this phenomenon, and we will explore them throughout the chapter.

Graphical Representation:

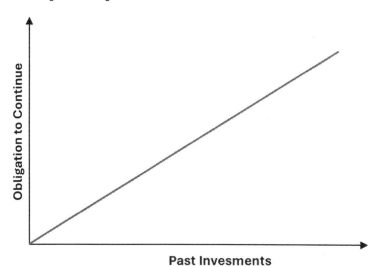

Graphical Key Points:

- The line demonstrates an increasing trend, indicating that the longer time is invested in a situation, the stronger the sense of obligation to continue.
- The line rises irrespective of the level of satisfaction in the situation; it doesn't influence the perceived obligation to continue.
- The graph encapsulates the essence of the Sunk Cost Fallacy, emphasizing the psychological conflict where past investments heavily influence decisions, often to the detriment of current happiness and well-being.

Life Scenario:

You're halfway through a college degree when you realize it's not the right fit for you or your career aspirations. However, you decide to continue it anyway, thinking about the time and money already spent, rather than switching to a more suitable field of study.

Wider Implications:

- **Personal Relationships:** Staying in a long-term relationship that has become unfulfilling, simply because of the years spent together.
- **Health and Fitness:** Sticking to a workout or diet plan that is not yielding results, just because of the time and effort already invested, despite better alternatives being available.
- **Business Strategy:** Deciding to continue a product line or service that no longer yields profit, even after substantial investment in its development and marketing.

Principle Origins:

Amos Tversky and Daniel Kahneman were the first to introduce the concept of cognitive biases in general in 1972, which laid the groundwork for understanding various biases, including the sunk cost fallacy. However, it was Richard Thaler who specifically introduced the term "Sunk Cost Fallacy" and began exploring it in detail in the 1980s, Thaler highlighted our tendency to continue a venture once an investment is made. Expanding on Thaler's work, Hal Arkes and Catherine Blumer conducted experiments in 1985 demonstrating how sunk costs influence decisions. In one study, participants were asked to choose between two ski trips they had accidentally booked for the same weekend: a $100 trip to Michigan and a $50 trip to Wisconsin. Despite being told they would enjoy the Wisconsin trip more, most chose the more expensive Michigan trip, demonstrating the sunk cost fallacy as they favored the option with the greater initial investment, even though it promised less enjoyment.

Analyzing the Principle:

- **Loss Aversion (Chapter 3):** The Sunk Cost Fallacy is closely tied to Loss Aversion, as it stems from our deep-seated fear of losing our investments, be they emotional, time-based, or financial. This bias occurs because acknowledging sunk costs as losses clashes with our instinct to avoid acknowledging losses, thus compelling us to irrationally continue unfavorable actions to mitigate feelings of waste and regret.
- **Cognitive Dissonance (Chapter 9):** Individuals might continue with a failing decision to reduce the dissonance between their belief in the decision's

potential success and the reality of its failure, rather than admitting the mistake and changing course.

- **The Framing Effect:** The Framing Effect is a cognitive bias where people's decisions are influenced by how information is presented, rather than just the information itself. If options are framed positively, individuals are more likely to be attracted to them, whereas a negative framing makes options less appealing. The Framing Effect influences how we perceive the value of continuing versus abandoning a project, when the option to continue is framed positively, we're more likely to view it as a success and persist, even if it's not the best decision. Conversely, the option to quit might be framed negatively, making us feel like we're admitting failure, which can push us to stick with a losing endeavor to avoid that perceived failure.

Insights to Implement in Life:

- **Embrace Adaptability:** In personal and professional life, being open to changes can prevent the sunk cost fallacy from taking hold. Be aware of why you are choosing to stay in any situation – is it due to past investments or present happiness? Don't stay on a sinking ship!
- **Set Clear Exit Criteria:** Before embarking on a new project or commitment, define specific conditions under which you would consider stopping or changing course. This proactive strategy helps prevent the sunk cost fallacy by providing a rational framework for decision-making.
- **Seek Objective Perspectives:** When you're too close to a situation, it's easy to get emotionally attached and

fall prey to the sunk cost fallacy. Consult with friends, family, or professionals who can provide unbiased advice, helping you to see the bigger picture and make more rational choices.

Summary:

The Sunk Cost Fallacy challenges us to reevaluate our commitments, not through the lens of past investments, but through the potential for future happiness and fulfillment. This fallacy can impair rational decision-making in various aspects of life by clouding judgment with emotional attachment to past efforts. Recognizing and overcoming this fallacy is crucial for making more objective and beneficial choices.

Chapter 25: The Decision Fatigue

"An hour in the morning is worth two in the evening."

Principle Introduction:

Decision fatigue is a psychological phenomenon where a person's ability to make decisions can deteriorate after a long session of decisions. Decision fatigue isn't just about the drop in decision quality as the day progresses, it's also about the cumulative effect of decisions over any period, whether that's during intense short meetings or throughout a long shopping session. Understanding this principle is crucial as it underscores the limits of our mental resources and the importance of managing them wisely.

Graphical Representation:

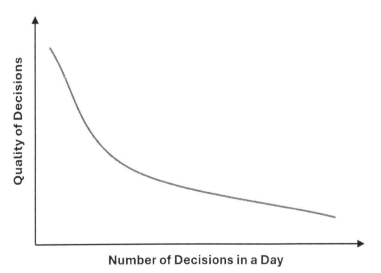

Graphical Key Points:

- When you start making decisions, the quality is high.
- The more decisions you make, the quality starts to go down.
- Even after lots of decisions, you still make choices, but the quality is much lower than at the beginning.

Life Scenario:

After choosing groceries for an hour at the supermarket, you reach the checkout and buy candies from the display, even though you are on a diet. Decision-making stamina is low after all the choices you've made, this is one of the supermarkets' strategies.

Wider Implications:

- **Event Planning:** When organizing a large event, from selecting the venue to the menu, after a full day of decision-making, even picking the color of napkins can seem daunting. The mind, already tired from the bigger decisions, now rebels against what should be a simple choice, leading to hasty decisions or the deferment of these minor but necessary details.
- **Relationship Timing:** In a relationship, timing can be everything when it comes to important conversations. Instead of bringing up sensitive topics late at night when decision fatigue has set in, couples could choose to discuss these matters during their peak decision-making times, typically in the morning or after a restful break. This approach ensures that both partners are mentally sharp and more likely to communicate effectively and make thoughtful decisions.

- **Investment Decisions:** For individuals managing their investment portfolios, the timing of decision-making can significantly impact on their financial health. Instead of making hasty investment choices after a long day of work, they might schedule time to review and make investment decisions when they are most alert and least susceptible to decision fatigue, ensuring more rational and well-considered choices.

Principle Origins:

In the late 1990s, notably in 1998, Roy Baumeister, along with his research team, conducted pivotal experiments to test the theory of ego depletion, which later laid the groundwork for understanding decision fatigue. In one seminal experiment, participants were asked to resist the temptation of cookies and chocolates, and afterward, they were tasked with solving unsolvable puzzles. The participants who exerted self-control to avoid the sweets exhibited signs of ego depletion and performed poorly on the subsequent problem-solving tasks. This finding led to the hypothesis that there is a limited reservoir of mental energy for exerting self-control and making decisions. Baumeister's work, particularly significant within fields that demand frequent and critical decision-making, emphasizes the necessity for strategic cognitive resource management to maintain high-quality decision-making capabilities.

Analyzing the Principle:

- **Cognitive Resource Allocation:** Like a battery charged by rest, our brain powers up with energy each morning. This energy gets spent as the day unfolds, sometimes leading to decision fatigue.

- **Emotional Decision-Making:** Emotions are powerful and can hijack our rational thinking, especially when we're tired. After making many decisions, we're more susceptible to emotional responses because our rational defenses are lower, which can lead to impulsive decisions.
- **Shining Optimism:** The vibrant morning light acts not just as a cue for our biological clock but also as a psychological booster. The brightness of morning is often associated with optimism and renewal, which can saturate our mindset, making us more likely to approach decisions with a positive outlook and a clearer, more hopeful perspective.

Insights to Implement in Life:

- **Simplify Morning Choices:** Reduce the mental load of everyday choices by establishing simple, consistent routines. A practical start is to standardize your attire – selecting a basic wardrobe with a low amount of options to bypass the daily fashion decision-making process. This strategy not only streamlines your morning but reserves cognitive energy for more significant decisions you'll encounter. This strategy of minimizing less consequential choices has been employed by notable figures such as Barack Obama and Mark Zuckerberg to maximize their focus on more impactful concerns.
- **Allocate Time for the Most Important Decisions:** Intentionally schedule a specific time of day for making important decisions when you are most alert. Avoid scheduling meetings that require strategic thinking later in the day when you are likely to experience decision fatigue.
- **Don't Overthink at Night!**

Summary:

Decision fatigue can lead to poorer choices as the day progresses, highlighting the need to prioritize and manage our decision-making energy. By understanding this principle and its implications, we can adapt our routines and habits to make the most of our mental resources, ensuring we make better choices throughout the day.

Chapter 26: Hick's Law

"More isn't always better. Sometimes it's just more."

– Barbara Benedek

Principle Introduction:

Hick's Law articulates a fundamental aspect of human decision-making: as the number of choices increases, so does the difficulty and time to decide which option is the best.

Graphical Representation:

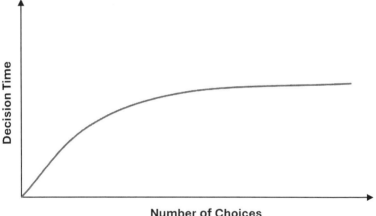

Graphical Key Points:

- Decision time increases as the number of choices grows.
- The rise in decision time slows down after a certain number of choices.

- Eventually, the decision time almost stays the same even if the number of choices continues to increase.

Life Scenario:

Imagine an ice cream shop with fifty flavors. You struggle to choose, feeling rushed as the line builds up behind you. Eventually, you pick one but keep wondering if another flavor was better. This indecision is a classic example of "choice paralysis." On the other hand, in a shop with fewer flavors, you'd likely make a quicker decision and enjoy your choice more, leading to a better overall experience.

Wider Implications:

- **Marketing:** Presenting a curated set of products to avoid overwhelming potential buyers.
- **Social Event Planning:** For event planning, offering fewer, well-chosen activities or menu options can make the planning process more manageable and the event more enjoyable for both the host and guests.
- **Healthcare Communication:** In healthcare, presenting patients with too many treatment options at once can be overwhelming.

Principle Origins:

Hick's Law, also known as the Hick-Hyman Law, was formulated by British psychologist William Edmund Hick and American psychologist Ray Hyman in the early 1950s. The law emerged from their research on the relationship between the number of stimuli presented to a person and their reaction time to decide which of the presented stimuli to choose. Hick observed that the reaction time increased logarithmically as the number of choices increased. Similarly, Hyman conducted experiments with different numbers of radio buttons and observed a similar pattern in the reaction time. By analyzing the data from these experiments, Hick and Hyman independently concluded that the time it takes for a person to make a decision increases logarithmically with the number of choices. The law is mainly named Hick's Law because William Edmund Hick's work was published earlier and became more widely recognized. Although Ray Hyman also contributed, Hick's name became more closely associated with the law over time.

Analyzing the Principle:

- **Paralysis by Analysis:** With more options, people tend to overthink and scrutinize every possible outcome, leading to decision paralysis. This phenomenon occurs because the fear of making wrong choice grows with more alternatives, causing stress and indecision.
- **Satisfaction Dilemma:** The more choices we have, the higher our expectations for the "perfect decision," which ironically can lead to lower satisfaction. This is due to the 'what if' factor – wondering without ever knowing if another choice would have been better creates a sense of regret, even if the decision made was a good one.
- **The Law of Diminishing Returns (Chapter 7):** Hick's Law serves as a specific example of the Law of Diminishing Returns in decision-making. There is a point beyond which adding more options yields diminishing benefits. In the context of Hick's Law, this point is reached when the addition of more choices no longer significantly improves decision quality but instead

increases the fear of making the wrong choice, heightens expectations for the perfect decision, and adds to the cognitive load.

Insights to Implement in Life:

- **Streamlined Choices:** Simplify your daily decisions by narrowing down options. Whether it's choosing what to wear, what to eat, or what movie to watch, pre-selecting a few choices can reduce decision fatigue and make your day smoother.
- **Prioritize Mindfully:** In any situation, identify the top priorities or most important factors to consider. This focused approach can help in making quicker, more effective decisions without being overwhelmed by less relevant details.
- **Pairwise Comparison for Complex Decisions:** When faced with a situation where you have many choices and can't reduce them, apply a modified approach inspired by Hick's Law. Break down your options into pairs and make a decision between each pair. This simplifies the decision-making process, as you're only comparing two options at a time, leading to shorter decision times. Then compare the winners in subsequent rounds until you have a final winner. This method helps manage cognitive load and streamline decision-making, even when the number of choices is unavoidably high.

Summary:

Hick's Law underscores the cognitive load involved in making decisions and offers a strategic approach to design and choice architecture. By minimizing choices and breaking down complex tasks, we can facilitate quicker, more satisfying decision-making experiences across a wide range of fields and domains.

Chapter 27: The Scarcity Principle

"Opportunities seem more valuable to us when their availability is limited."

Principle Introduction:

The Scarcity Principle, a fundamental concept in economics and psychology, posits that limited availability increases an item's perceived value. This principle influences human behavior, driving us to desire and prioritize scarce resources or opportunities more than those readily available. It highlights how scarcity can heighten appeal, motivate action, and shape decision-making.

Graphical Representation:

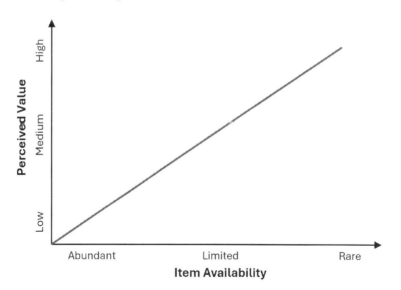

Graphical Key Points:

- The graph starts with items that are abundant, which are perceived as less valuable.
- As items become less available, their perceived value begins to rise.
- When items are rare, their perceived value is the highest, showing that scarcity is closely linked to higher value.

Life Scenario:

The launch of a brand's limited-edition sneaker turns into an event, with eager fans queuing for hours and resellers capitalizing on the hype, as the sneaker's rarity makes it a coveted item, skyrocketing its market value.

Wider Implications:

- **Personal Relationships:** Scarcity can influence personal relationships, with scarce attention or affection increasing its perceived value in interpersonal interactions.
- **Marketing Strategies:** Businesses use scarcity tactics, such as limited time offers or exclusive products, to drive consumer interest and sales.
- **Employee Retention:** In the corporate world, presenting opportunities for advancement as rare and valuable can make them more sought-after, motivating employees to excel and remain with the company.

Principle Origins:

The Scarcity Principle, particularly in the context of psychology, was notably explored by Robert Cialdini in his foundational research on the psychology of persuasion. In his seminal book, "Influence: The Psychology of Persuasion," published in 1984, Cialdini delved into the mechanisms behind the principle of scarcity and its impact on human behavior. He conducted various experiments to demonstrate how the perceived scarcity of an item or opportunity can significantly increase its attractiveness and desirability. For instance, in one experiment, participants were more inclined to purchase products that were advertised as being in limited supply or available for a limited time. Cialdini's research highlighted the powerful role of scarcity in influencing decision-making, leading to the conclusion that opportunities seem more valuable when their availability is limited.

Analyzing the Principle:

- **The Novelty Factor:** Rare items often carry an air of uniqueness. Owning or experiencing something rare makes us feel special and can become a part of our identity. Much like a rare stamp in a collection, the scarcity of an object or experience can confer a sense of distinction and pride to its possessor.
- **Fear of Missing Out (FOMO):** Scarcity triggers a psychological response where individuals fear missing out on opportunities, driving them to make hasty decisions, as the urgency created by limited availability pressures individuals to act swiftly.
- **Anticipation and Excitement:** Scarcity can elevate anticipation, turning the wait for a product or experience into a part of the allure. Just as a limited theatrical run makes a play more exciting to attend, scarcity heightens our emotional investment in obtaining the desired object.

Insights to Implement in Life:

- **Evaluate Scarcity Claims:** Be mindful of artificial scarcity created to manipulate your behavior. Assess whether the scarcity is genuine or a marketing tactic.
- **Balance Urgency with Rationality:** Even after successfully identifying the scarcity principle in action, it can still create a sense of urgency. Actively hold yourself from making impulsive decisions, take the time to evaluate the true value and necessity of the scarce item.
- **Create Value Through Scarcity:** If you're offering a product or service, consider how limited availability or exclusive access can enhance its appeal to your target audience.

Summary:

The Scarcity Principle powerfully influences decision-making by making us value what's less available. Understanding this can guide smarter choices, helping businesses create demand and individuals to discern true value, ensuring decisions are driven by genuine worth rather than mere rarity.

Chapter 28: Fredkin's Paradox

"The smaller the difference, the bigger the hesitation."

Principle Introduction:

Fredkin's Paradox brings out an obvious but also peculiar truth about how we make choices: the more two options look alike, the harder it gets to choose one. It shows us that we often spend too much time thinking over small decisions.

Graphical Representation:

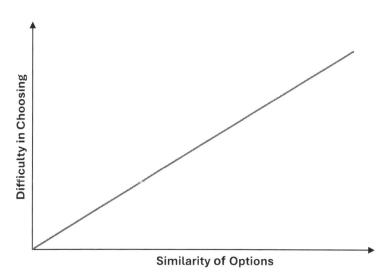

Graphical Key Points:

- When options are different, choosing is easier.
- As the similarity of options increases, choosing gets harder.

- When options are very alike, it's much harder to choose.

Life Scenario:

As a book lover with a long reading list, you find it surprisingly difficult to pick your next read when several books are equally appealing. The more you try to compare them based on reviews, genres, and recommendations, the more indecisive you become.

Wider Implications:

- **Breakfast Routine:** Deciding each morning between two nearly identical breakfast cereals without realizing the choice has minimal impact on your day.
- **Shopping:** Choosing between two similar smartphones with nearly identical features, even though your daily usage will be largely unaffected by the minor differences.
- **Travel Planning:** Deciding between two similar beach destinations for a weekend getaway, although both offer the relaxation you seek.

Principle Origins:

Fredkin's Paradox is named after Edward Fredkin, a physicist and computer scientist who contributed significantly to the field of digital physics. The paradox itself does not originate from a specific foundational research study or experiment but rather from Fredkin's observations and theoretical work in the mid-20th century, particularly around the 1960s and 1970s. Fredkin's Paradox highlights the counterintuitive nature of decision-making, where individuals often find it more difficult to choose between two nearly identical options than between two clearly distinct ones. This concept has implications in various fields, including psychology, economics, and computer science, especially in understanding human and machine decision-making processes.

Analyzing the Principle:

- **Decisional Contrasts:** The bias may stem from our brain's desire for clear contrasts to make swift decisions. When options are too similar, our cognitive mechanism lacks the contrast it needs, leading to prolonged decision-making as it searches for a distinguishing factor.
- **Fear of Regret:** Psychologically, we dread the feeling of regret. Similar choices amplify this fear, as making a 'wrong' choice seems more probable when differences are small. We're wired to avoid potential regret, which paradoxically leads to more indecision.
- **Analysis Paralysis:** The more homogenous the options, the deeper we dive into analysis, looking for the best possible choice. This can create a loop of constant comparison and second-guessing, reflecting our cognitive bias towards optimizing even the most trivial of decisions.

Insights to Implement in Life:

- **Trust Your Initial Instincts:** When faced with similar options, pay attention to your initial instincts. Often, your first reaction is a reflection of your true preferences and values. By trusting and acting on these instincts, you can navigate through the decision-making process

more swiftly and confidently, minimizing the indecision that arises from Fredkin's Paradox.
- **Consider Overlooked Factors:** When evaluating similar options, it's easy to focus on the most obvious criteria and overlook other important factors that can potentially have significant differences for each of the options. Take a step back and consider aspects such as the potential for personal growth, the impact on your mental health, or how each choice aligns with your long-term goals. Broadening your perspective can help you make more informed decisions and avoid the paralysis of Fredkin's Paradox.
- **Set Decision Time Limits:** To avoid overthinking when faced with similar options, set a strict time limit for your decision-making process. When the time is up, commit to one of the choices and continue your day. This approach helps you avoid getting bogged down in minor details and ensures that you make timely decisions without unnecessary delay.

Summary:

Fredkin's Paradox shows us a funny side of human nature: we sometimes make a big deal out of small things. By understanding this, we can get better at making decisions without wasting time on the little differences that don't really matter.

Chapter 29: The Endowment Effect

"People value things more highly as soon as they own them."

Principle Introduction:

The Endowment Effect is a cognitive bias that causes people to ascribe more value to things merely because they own them. Coined by economist Richard Thaler, it challenges traditional market theories by showing how ownership influences perceived value, often irrationally.

Graphical Representation:

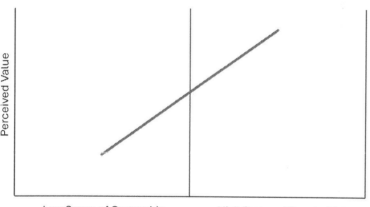

Graphical Key Points:

- A notable increase in perceived value occurs once ownership is established.
- The effect may diminish backward if the item is no longer owned.

- This bias is not necessarily related to the actual utility or quality of the item, only to the sense of ownership and belonging.

Life Scenario:

Imagine a homeowner who has dedicated years to maintaining his home. Due to his emotional attachment and the personalized touches he has added, he believes his home is worth more than its market value. However, he is surprised to find that when he decides to sell the house, no one is willing to pay the price he believes it is worth.

Wider Implications:

- **Social media:** Platforms use the Endowment Effect by allowing users to customize their profiles and content, creating a sense of ownership and increasing user attachment and activity.
- **Parental Attachment:** The Endowment Effect explains parts of the intense love parents have for their children. It suggests that the deep emotional investment in their offspring creates a strong sense of attachment, leading parents to value their children's well-being and happiness above all else.
- **Consumer Behavior:** Explains phenomena like reluctance to switch brands or try new products.

Principle Origins:

The Endowment Effect was first experimentally demonstrated by Richard Thaler, Daniel Kahneman, and Jack Knetsch in a series of studies in the late 1980s and early 1990s. One of their most notable experiments took place in 1990, where participants were randomly divided into buyers, sellers, and choosers. Sellers were given a mug and asked at what price they would be willing to sell it, while buyers were asked at what price they would be willing to buy the same mug. Choosers were asked whether they would prefer the mug or an equivalent amount of money. The results showed that sellers valued the mug approximately twice as much as the buyers, demonstrating the Endowment Effect. In addition, the choosers' valuations were similar to those of the buyers, indicating that ownership significantly increased the sellers' perceived value of the mug. This discrepancy between willingness to accept and willingness to pay highlighted the psychological impact of ownership on perceived value, challenging traditional economic theories that assumed rational behavior and consistent value assessment.

Analyzing the Principle:

- **Loss Aversion (Chapter 3):** When faced with the prospect of parting with an item, the potential loss feels more significant than the potential gain of selling or exchanging it. This discrepancy leads to the inflated valuation of personal possessions, as owners weigh the emotional cost of losing the item more heavily than its objective market value.
- **Sense of Identity:** Objects we own often become intertwined with our sense of self and identity. Letting go of these items can feel like losing a part of oneself, which is why people might assign a higher value to them. This attachment can be especially strong for items that hold sentimental value or are associated with significant life events.

- **Effort Justification:** According to this psychological theory, the more effort we put into something, the more we value it. This can explain why people might overvalue items they have invested time and energy in, such as a DIY project or a collection they have curated over years.

Insights to Implement in Life:

- **Embrace Detachment:** Practice letting go of material possessions that no longer serve a purpose or bring joy. This can be achieved through regular decluttering sessions or mindful reflection on the true value of items. By embracing detachment, you can create space for new experiences and reduce the hold of the Endowment Effect on your decision-making.
- **Enhanced Negotiation Skills:** Awareness of the Endowment Effect can be beneficial in scenarios like buying a house. The seller might overvalue the property due to personal attachment. Recognizing this bias, you can negotiate more effectively, presenting data on comparable market prices to counter their inflated valuation. Conversely, knowing you might overvalue your own assets, like a piece of inherited furniture, can prevent you from demanding an unreasonable price when selling.
- **Seek External Perspectives:** When making decisions about keeping or letting go of possessions, seek advice from trusted friends or family members. An external perspective can provide a more objective view, helping you to overcome the bias of the Endowment Effect and make more rational choices.

Summary:

The Endowment Effect is a fascinating psychological phenomenon that reveals how we often overvalue what we own, simply because it's ours. By understanding this effect, we can unlock the door to more rational decision-making and skillful negotiation, seeing past the veil of ownership to assess true value. Embracing detachment, cultivating gratitude, and seeking external perspectives are key strategies to overcome this bias. So, the next time you're holding onto something a little too tightly, remember the Endowment Effect, and ask yourself: "Do I really value this, or is it just the ownership talking?"

Chapter 30: The Balance of Heart and Mind Interactive Chapter 4

"When emotion goes up, intelligence goes down."

Graphical Representation:

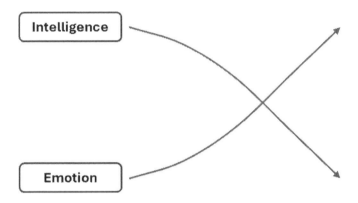

Reflective Exercise:

As you gaze upon the graph before you, take a moment to recall instances where the heart's whisper overpowered the mind's roar. Ask yourself:
- How have your feelings affected your thinking during tough choices, did you notice that?
- Remember when strong emotions led you off course or brought unexpected happiness?

Closing Thought:

In decision-making, maintaining a balance between emotions and rational thinking is crucial. This balance can shift rapidly and often goes unnoticed. While it's essential to be in a mental state unaffected by intense emotions that could skew the process, the key is to recognize when you're in an emotionally charged state and avoid making decisions during those situations.

Part 5
The Emotional Graphs

"The heart has its reasons which reason knows not."

– Blaise Pascal

In this part, we explore the emotional graphs that map the contours of our hearts. We'll navigate through the complex terrain of happiness, sadness, love, and the many shades of emotions that define our human experience. As we journey through these graphs, you'll discover the profound ways in which our emotions influence our thoughts, actions, and the very fabric of our lives. Prepare to connect deeply with the emotional currents that flow within you and uncover the power they hold in shaping your world.

Chapter 31: The Hedonic Treadmill

"Happiness is not a station you arrive at, but a manner of traveling."

– Margaret Lee Runbeck

Principle Introduction:

The Hedonic Treadmill, also known as hedonic adaptation, is a psychological phenomenon where an individual's level of happiness eventually stabilizes, regardless of significant positive or negative life changes. It's like running on a treadmill – you work hard but not really moving forward emotionally, this concept suggests that people have a baseline level of happiness to which they return, despite fluctuations in life circumstances.

Graphical Representation:

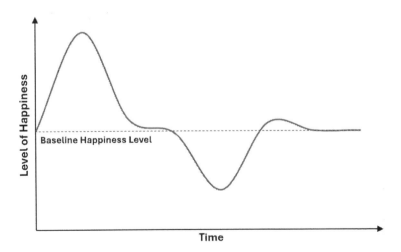

Graphical Key Points:

- Initial spikes in happiness levels following positive life events (like winning a lottery).
- Drops in happiness following negative life events (such as a personal loss).
- Gradual return to a baseline level of happiness over time.

Life Scenario:

After years of hard work, you receive a well-deserved promotion at work. You feel a sense of achievement and pride, and your colleagues congratulate you on your success. As the weeks go by, the challenges and responsibilities of the new position become the norm. The initial boost in happiness you felt from the promotion gradually diminishes, and you find yourself back on the hedonic treadmill, perhaps already thinking about the next step in your career.

Wider Implications:

- **Fitness Goals:** You reach your fitness goal, whether it's losing weight or running a marathon. You're enthusiastic at first, but eventually, this achievement becomes your new norm, and the sense of accomplishment diminishes.
- **Relationship Building:** Applying the principle to relationships, couples can focus on creating consistently shared experiences and open communication to maintain a deeper connection, rather than relying solely on initial romance.
- **Home Renovation:** You remodel your kitchen, and for a while, you feel thrilled every time you walk in. Over

time, the newness wears off, and it feels like part of your normal living space.

Principle Origins:

The concept of the hedonic treadmill was first introduced by psychologists Brickman and Campbell in their 1971 paper, "Hedonic Relativism and Planning the Good Society." They conducted studies on lottery winners and found that while these individuals experienced an initial surge of happiness following their windfall, their overall happiness levels returned to baseline after a relatively short period. This observation led to the conclusion that people adapt to changes in their circumstances, whether positive or negative, and their overall level of happiness tends to revert to a stable set point over time. This phenomenon has been further explored and validated in various studies, reinforcing the idea that external events have a temporary impact on our happiness.

Analyzing the Principle:

- **Natural Adaptation:** Humans have a remarkable ability to adapt to both positive and negative changes in their lives. This adaptation helps us maintain emotional stability in the face of varying circumstances. It also means that the happiness we derive from new experiences or possessions tends to diminish over time.
- **Neurochemical Factors:** Our brains release Dopamine, a "feel-good" neurotransmitter, in response to new experiences or rewards. However, over time, our brains adapt to these stimuli, and the same experiences no longer trigger the same level of Dopamine release, leading to a return to our baseline happiness.

- **The Influence of Maturity:** As people mature, simply by getting used to life's ups and downs, their emotional responses become more moderated, which is reflected in smaller variations from their baseline happiness level. This might be because mature individuals have a clearer sense of what brings them lasting satisfaction, or a more philosophical approach to life's inevitable changes.

Insights to Implement in Life:

- **Recognizing Adaptation:** Understanding that happiness levels adapt over time can provide an optimistic and mature perspective during life's highs and lows.
- **Elevating Baseline Happiness level:** Shifting focus from achieving external events goals (like getting a promotion, buying a new car, or going on vacation) into focusing on internal growth and self-development goals (like continuously learning new skills, family time, and physical activity) to enhance your baseline happiness level.
- **Invest in Relationships:** Prioritize meaningful relationships and connections. Investing time and energy in building and nurturing relationships with family, friends, and community can provide a more stable and enduring source of happiness.

Summary:

The Hedonic Treadmill illustrates the human tendency to return to a stable level of happiness regardless of external circumstances. Acknowledging this can help individuals seek more sustainable forms of happiness and well-being, focusing on internal growth and appreciating life's journey rather than its milestones.

Chapter 32: The Happiness-Income Correlation

"Money can't buy happiness, but neither can poverty."

– Leo Rosten

Principle Introduction:

While traditional wisdom suggests that money can't buy happiness, recent research led by Daniel Kahneman, Matthew A. Killingsworth, and Barbara Mellers unveils a more nuanced reality. Disputing earlier assumptions, they found that happiness extends even beyond certain income levels, growing steadily, though more subtly, with wealth. This revelation invites a deeper exploration into how financial prosperity influences our sense of fulfillment. This chapter seeks to unravel the evolving narrative surrounding the complex interplay between wealth and emotional well-being, offering fresh perspectives on an age-old debate.

Graphical Representation:

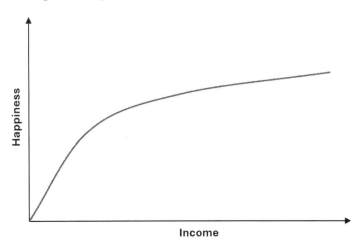

Graphical Key Points:

- The graph starts with a steep initial climb where increases in income correlate with significant gains in happiness, likely due to the fulfillment of basic needs and security.
- After reaching a certain income level, the rate of happiness rise slows down, without necessarily flattening entirely.
- The specific point at which happiness slows down with income increase can vary among individuals, as it is influenced by personal circumstances, values, and the definition of happiness itself.

Life Scenario:

Consider three neighbors with contrasting lifestyles. The first neighbor works in a high-paying job, enjoys luxury vacations once a year, and always seeks the next expensive purchase, although because of his job he doesn't have much time for his family. The second neighbor, earning less, runs a small business and values time in nature and with family over material wealth. The third neighbor earns more than the first neighbor and can afford to work only 4 hours a day, spending the rest of the time with his family and friends, finding contentment in life's simple and grand joys whenever he wants. Who do you think is the happiest?

Wider Implications:

- **Health and Wellness:** Investing in health and wellness is a direct application of how money can contribute to happiness. This includes access to quality healthcare, nutritious food, regular fitness activities,

and mental health support. These investments lead to improved physical and mental health, which is foundational to happiness.
- **Education and Personal Growth:** Money can unlock opportunities for education and personal development. Whether it's pursuing higher education, acquiring new skills, or indulging in hobbies, these activities enrich the mind, open new career paths, and enhance one's sense of fulfillment and self-worth.
- **Philanthropy and Giving Back:** Studies show that the ability to donate or help those in need can elevate mood and provide profound satisfaction and purpose.

Principle Origins:

The principle of the happiness-income correlation has been a topic of debate for decades. Early studies suggested a linear relationship, with happiness increasing as income rose. However, the 2010 study by Kahneman and Deaton introduced a groundbreaking concept: a happiness plateau beyond an income threshold, specifically around $75,000 annually. In 2023, a new study by Kahneman, Killingsworth, and Mellers revisited this theory, utilizing a larger dataset and advanced methodologies. Surprisingly, their results contradicted the earlier findings, showing that happiness continues to grow with income, albeit at a slower rate, but without flattening entirely.

Analyzing the Principle:

- **Maslow's Hierarchy of Needs:** This theory suggests that human needs are arranged in levels from material to psychological. Initially, individuals seek to fulfill

basic needs like food and shelter, this explains why the correlation starts the fastest. Once these are met, they move on to psychological needs such as belonging and esteem. The highest level, self-actualization, is about achieving one's full potential. The psychological needs that come afterwards, which are not directly tied to income, are often obtained easier without the distress of money.
- **Opportunity for Experiences:** This may seem obvious but needs to be emphasized. Money can buy experiences that lead to lasting happiness, such as travel, education, and cultural activities, which enrich one's life and create cherished memories. The more money you have, the more opportunities you will have for these experiences.
- **The Hedonic Treadmill (Chapter 31) and the Law of Diminishing Returns (Chapter 7):** As discussed in previous chapters, individuals quickly adapt to increased happiness, often as a result of higher income. This, along with the law of diminishing returns, creates a distinct pattern: Each additional dollar earned brings progressively less happiness than the previous one. This will probably ultimately lead to a plateau in the relationship between income and happiness. However, there isn't any scientific evidence in the 2023 study that shows this plateau until incomes of $500,000, and beyond this point, there wasn't enough data to determine.

Insights to Implement in Life:

- **Meet Basic Needs First:** Ensure that your fundamental needs are met before focusing on higher-level

aspirations. This solid foundation features the highest rate of the happiness-income correlation.
- **Remember that the Richest is not necessarily the Happiest:** Prioritizing well-being sometimes means choosing work-life balance over a promotion with increased salary. Reflect with yourself which choice will ultimately bring you more happiness and fulfillment before accepting increased responsibilities that may lead to stress and burnout.
- **Embrace Financial Literacy Early on:** Understanding the power of compound interest (Chapter 8) is just the beginning. Prioritize financial literacy from an early age. Learn how to budget, save, invest, and manage debt effectively. Solid foundation in financial knowledge can lead to smarter financial decisions, increased wealth over time, and ultimately more happiness.

Summary:

The fresh understanding of the happiness-income correlation invites us to reconsider our approach to money and happiness. It suggests that while money is not the sole determinant of happiness, it plays a significant role even beyond certain thresholds. This chapter encourages a balanced pursuit of financial and personal growth for a fulfilling life.

Chapter 33: The Kübler-Ross Model

"Grief is itself a medicine."

– William Cowper

Principle Introduction:

The Kübler-Ross Model, also known as the five stages of grief, outlines a progression of emotional states experienced by those who face significant life changes or loss. Originally conceptualized to understand the grieving process associated with death, the model has since been generalized to a variety of emotional upheavals. This chapter will chart the course of these emotional stages, reflecting on their universal applicability and the insights they offer into the human condition.

Graphical Representation:

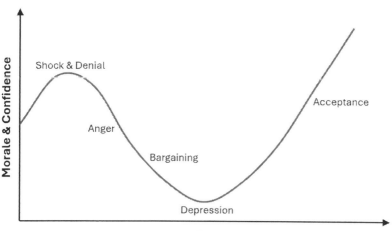

Graphical Key Points:

- **Denial:** In this initial stage, individuals often experience shock and disbelief, struggling to accept the reality of the situation. It serves as a defense mechanism to help buffer the immediate impact of the loss.
- **Anger:** As the denial fades, the reality and pain of the situation become more apparent, leading to feelings of anger and frustration. This anger can be directed at others, oneself, or even the situation itself.
- **Bargaining:** To regain control or find a way out of the situation, individuals may engage in bargaining, often with a higher power. This stage is characterized by thoughts like "If only I had done this differently..." or "If only I can get through this..."
- **Depression:** As the reality of the situation settles in, individuals may experience deep sadness, hopelessness, and a sense of loss. This stage reflects the mourning process for what has been lost.
- **Acceptance:** In this final stage, individuals come to terms with the reality of their situation. Acceptance doesn't mean happiness, but rather a sense of peace and the ability to move forward.

Life Scenario:

The sudden end to a cherished relationship can trigger the journey through the Kübler-Ross stages, from the initial disbelief and denial to the final acceptance and moving on.

Wider Implications:

- **Career Disruption:** An unexpected career setback, such as a job loss, can initiate the progression through these emotional stages.

- **Personal Dream Adjustment:** The relinquishing of a long-held personal dream or goal, such as an athlete facing an injury that ends their career, can mirror the stages as they come to terms with a new reality.
- **Social Movements:** Recognizing the collective emotional journey in response to social or political upheaval.

Principle Origins:

The Kübler-Ross Model was proposed by Elisabeth Kübler-Ross in her 1969 book "On Death and Dying," based on her work with terminally ill patients. The model has become a seminal framework for understanding the process of grieving, not just for those who are dying, but for anyone experiencing a significant loss.

Analyzing the Principle:

- **Emotional Cycle of Change (Chapter 10):** The Kübler-Ross Model aligns with the Emotional Cycle of Change in the sense that both frameworks describe a journey through emotional states. While the Kübler-Ross Model focuses on the response to loss, the Emotional Cycle of Change addresses emotions during intentional transformations.
- **Neurobiological Underpinnings:** Recent research has started to uncover the neurobiological underpinnings of the grieving process. For example, studies using neuroimaging techniques have shown that the experience of loss can activate brain regions associated with physical pain, stress, and attachment. This suggests that grief is not only an emotional response but also a complex physiological process that affects the brain and body.

- **Personal Timelines:** The model is not rigid, many people may not experience every stage, and may revisit stages in a non-linear fashion.

Insights to Implement in Life:

- **Acknowledge Your Feelings:** It's important to recognize and accept your emotions, whether it's denial, anger, bargaining, depression, or acceptance. Understand that it's natural to have a range of feelings during this time, and allowing yourself to experience them fully is a crucial part of the healing process.
- **Be Patient with Yourself:** Healing takes time, and there's no set timeline for grieving. Give yourself permission to move through the stages at your own pace, without rushing or forcing yourself to feel a certain way.
- **Empathetic Engagement:** Recognizing these stages in others can improve your ability to support them with empathy and compassion.

Summary:

The Kübler-Ross Model offers an inspiring guide to understanding our emotional responses to significant life changes. By recognizing the stages of this journey, we unlock the potential for greater self-awareness, compassion, and strength. It's a valuable tool that empowers us to approach life's shifts with empathy, patience, and a resilient spirit. Importantly, it highlights the beautiful capacity we must have in order to adapt and grow through change, culminating in heightened morale and confidence at the end of the journey.

Chapter 34: The Romantic Fantasy Effect

"Fantasy love is much better than reality love."

– Andy Warhol

Principle Introduction:

The Romantic Fantasy Effect delves into the intriguing psychological pattern where less information about a person leads to greater romantic attraction. This principle reflects the human tendency to idealize and fill in unknowns with hopeful imagination.

Graphical Representation:

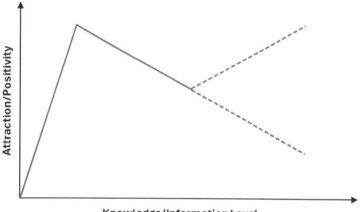

Graphical Key Points:

- Initial steep rise in attraction with minimal knowledge and peak of romanticized attraction even before mid-level knowledge.

- Small descending as real knowledge breaks fantasies.
- As someone learns more, their level of attraction to something or someone can change significantly, either becoming stronger or weaker.

Life Scenario:

On dating apps, the Romantic Fantasy Effect unfolds as individuals idealize their matches with limited information. Surprisingly, those with less detailed initial profiles often receive more matches, fueling elevated hopes and expectations. However, as they communicate and learn more about each other, the initial idealization often gives way to a more realistic view of their potential partner.

Wider Implications:

- **Marketing and consumer behavior:** Less information can lead to idealized product expectations.
- **Celebrities:** Celebrities are often idealized by fans who see them as perfect and flawless. However, as more information about celebrities comes to light, fans may see a more realistic view of who they are.
- **Politics:** New political candidates are often idealized by voters, who project high hopes and expectations onto them based on campaign promises and limited information (The Scarcity principle – Chapter 28). However, as candidates assume office and face the complexities of governance, this initial idealization can fade, revealing a more realistic view of their capabilities and limitations.

Principle Origins:

The Romantic Fantasy Effect can be traced back to psychological theories that explore how people fill in missing information with idealized assumptions. Research in the 1990s led by social psychologists like Robert Knox examined how individuals idealize their partners in long-distance relationships, coining the term "absence makes the heart grow fonder." This early work laid the groundwork for understanding how limited information leads to romantic idealization, a concept that has evolved into the Romantic Fantasy Effect in the context of modern dating, particularly with the rise of online dating platforms.

Analyzing the Principle:

- **Imagination and Idealization:** Our imagination fills in gaps with positive traits and characteristics, creating an attractive fantasy. It occurs because our minds naturally seek to make sense of incomplete information and tend to lean towards positive interpretations.
- **Curiosity and Mystery:** The allure of the unknown and curiosity about someone's hidden qualities can intensify romantic attraction. The desire to uncover more about a person, coupled with the anticipation of discovering positive traits, fuels the initial fantasy. It occurs because humans are naturally drawn to novelty and the excitement of exploration.
- **The Halo Effect:** The Romantic Fantasy Effect is related to psychological theories like the "Halo Effect," where a positive impression of one aspect of a person's character leads to an overly favorable view of their

overall character. In dating apps for example, if someone finds a user's photo attractive, they might assume that the person is also kind, successful and fun, even without any evidence to support this assumption.

Insights to Implement in Life:

- **Embrace the Balance Between Idealization and Reality:** In relationships, it's natural to start with a sense of idealization, especially when information is limited. However, as you get to know someone, allow yourself to transition from the initial fantasy to embracing the real person, with all their strengths and flaws. This balance is key to forming deeper, more authentic connections that are based on understanding and acceptance rather than just surface-level attraction.
- **Strategic First Impression:** In the early stages of dating or networking, you can use the Romantic Fantasy Effect to your advantage by carefully curating the information you share about yourself. Present a compelling, but not overly detailed, version of yourself to spark interest and curiosity. This allows the other person to fill in the gaps with positive assumptions, creating an initial allure. However, be sure to gradually reveal more authentic details about yourself as the relationship progresses to build a foundation of trust and genuine connection.
- **Managing Expectations in Business Settings:** In professional environments, you can apply the Romantic Fantasy Effect by setting realistic expectations when presenting projects or proposals. Initially, provide enough intriguing information to capture interest and stimulate imagination, but avoid overpromising.

As discussions advance, offer more detailed insights and data to ground expectations. This approach can help maintain enthusiasm while ensuring that the final outcome meets or exceeds the initially perceived potential.

Summary:

The Romantic Fantasy Effect captures a common psychological phenomenon affecting our perception of others, especially in the context of romance. By understanding this effect, we can navigate our social and romantic lives more mindfully, distinguishing between the allure of the unknown and the reality of the known.

Chapter 35: The Ben Franklin Effect

"He that has once done you a kindness will be more ready to do you another, than he whom you yourself have obliged."

– Benjamin Franklin

Principle Introduction:

The Ben Franklin Effect stands as a subtle yet profound testament to human psychology. It suggests that when we do someone a favor, we tend to like them more as a result. This counterintuitive insight defies the expectation that we favor those who help us, proposing instead that our affections grow when we invest effort into others.

Graphical Representation:

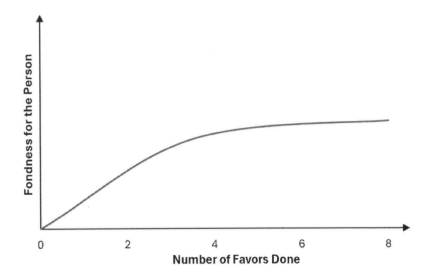

Graphical Key Points:

- As the number of favors done increases, so does the fondness and affection for the person.
- There's a consistent upward trend in affection with each additional favor.
- The growth in affection slows down after a certain amount of favors, which can differ between individuals.

Life Scenario:

Imagine volunteering to help a colleague with a project. As you invest time and effort, you find your opinion of them improving. This personal growth in your view of the colleague illustrates the Ben Franklin Effect in action.

Wider Implications:

- **Sports Coaching:** Coaches asking players to help with team strategy can increase mutual respect and friendship within the team.
- **Business Negotiations:** Companies asking for input from their clients on service improvement can lead to stronger client-company relationships.
- **Travel Planning:** Travelers who help others plan their trips often find greater enjoyment and personal investment in the travel experiences of others.

Principle Origins:

The Ben Franklin Effect stems from an incident in the 18th century during Benjamin Franklin's early political career when he asked a rival legislator to lend him a rare book. After lending the book, Franklin noticed that the legislator's attitude towards him changed significantly, becoming more friendly and supportive. This anecdote was later studied and validated by researchers in the 1960s, specifically in an experiment conducted by Jecker and Landy. In their experiment, students participated in a Q&A competition with a chance to win money. After the competition, some students were asked by the researcher to return the money due to a shortage of funds, while others were asked by a secretary or not approached at all. When asked about their liking for the researcher, those who were directly asked to return the money by the researcher liked him the most, demonstrating the Ben Franklin effect.

Analyzing the Principle:

- **Cognitive Dissonance (Chapter 9):** When someone does a favor for another person, they may experience cognitive dissonance if they don't particularly like that person. To resolve this discomfort, their brain rationalizes the action by increasing their liking for the person they helped. This aligns their beliefs with their actions, reducing dissonance.
- **Social Exchange Theory:** This theory suggests that social interactions are based on an exchange process where individuals seek to maximize rewards and minimize costs. When someone does a favor for another person, they may perceive it as an investment in the relationship, expecting that it will lead to positive outcomes in the future, such as reciprocal favors, increased social status, or stronger social bonds. This expectation of future benefits can enhance the likability of the person for whom the favor was done.

- **Increased Familiarity:** When someone does a favor for another person, it often leads to increased interactions and communication between the two parties. This increased familiarity can lead to a greater sense of comfort and liking. Humans are generally more inclined to have positive feelings towards those they are familiar with, so the act of doing a favor can naturally lead to a more favorable view of the person being helped.

Insights to Implement in Life:

- **Bridge Building:** If you're not on great terms with someone, ask them for a small, easily achievable favor. It's a non-confrontational way to initiate positive interaction and can lead to a thawing of icy relations.
- **Encourage Mutual Assistance:** Ask for small favors during your first meetings and show you're open to help in return. This fosters a reciprocal, positive connection from the start.
- **Be Mindful of Manipulation:** While the Ben Franklin Effect can be a powerful tool for building positive relationships, it's important to be cautious of situations where it might be used manipulatively. If reciprocating favors makes you uncomfortable, reassess the situation. True relationships thrive on mutual respect, not on calculating favors. Trust your instincts and stick to your values.

Summary:

The Ben Franklin Effect invites us to reconsider the dynamics of our social interactions and personal feelings. It teaches that through giving, not just receiving, we forge deeper connections and nurture our own growth and well-being. However, be cautious – if you've built a good relationship with someone using the Ben Franklin effect, don't keep asking for favors endlessly, you might turn the friendship into a lifelong game of hide-and-seek.

Chapter 36: The Hedgehog's Dilemma

"Intimacy requires courage because risk is inescapable. We cannot know at the outset how the relationship will affect us."

– Rollo May

Principle Introduction:

The Hedgehogs' Dilemma metaphorically illustrates the challenges of human intimacy. It suggests that despite a mutual need for closeness, the closer we get to someone, the more we can inadvertently hurt each other.

Graphical Representation:

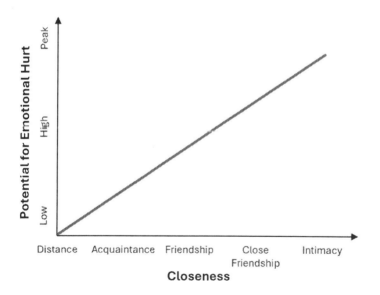

Graphical Key Points:

- **Distance:** Low potential for emotional hurt due to minimal closeness.
- **Linear Correlation:** Elevated potential for emotional hurt with increased closeness.
- **Intimacy:** Highest potential for emotional hurt at maximum closeness.

Life Scenario:

In a new romantic relationship, two individuals initially enjoy the thrill of discovery and the joy of connecting on a deep level. As they share more of themselves, they become emotionally invested, but this also increases the fear of potential heartbreak. The Hedgehog's Dilemma is evident as they navigate the delicate balance between opening up to deepen the bond and protecting their hearts from the possibility of being hurt. The challenge lies in allowing themselves to be vulnerable to experience love fully, while also being mindful of the risks involved. Embracing this vulnerability can lead to a deeper, more meaningful connection, where the rewards of love outweigh the fears of emotional hurt.

Wider Implications:

- **Friendships:** New friendships blossom as individuals share personal tales, embracing vulnerability to foster deeper connections.
- **Professional Relationships:** In the workplace, colleagues strive for teamwork, navigating the delicate balance between trust and the risk of betrayal that could affect their professional achievements.

- **Family Dynamics:** Family members balancing closeness with personal boundaries, managing conflicts while striving to maintain harmony and support.

Principle Origins:

The concept, often attributed to the philosopher Arthur Schopenhauer, is derived from a parable about hedgehogs who struggle to find a comfortable closeness to keep warm without hurting each other with their spines. It has been used in psychology to describe the human condition of seeking intimacy but facing the inevitable challenges it brings.

Analyzing the Principle:

- **Instinctive Self-Protection:** Psychologically, individuals are wired to protect themselves from potential threats, including emotional harm. This can lead to the creation of defense mechanisms that keep others at a safe distance, much like a hedgehog's spines.
- **Social Need for Belonging:** Humans are social creatures with an innate desire to belong and form connections. This drive is so strong that it can override the fear of potential hurt, compelling us to seek closeness despite the risks.
- **Personal Trauma and Past Experiences:** Individual histories of pain, betrayal, or loss can heighten the fear of vulnerability, making the Hedgehog's Dilemma more pronounced, and to intensify the slope of the graph as a result.

Insights to Implement in Life:

- **Love Outweighs Fear:** In the realm of love, remember that the potential for deep, rewarding connections

often outweighs the fear of emotional hurt. Embracing this can empower you to approach relationships with optimism and openness, leading to more fulfilling experiences.
- **Gradual Relationship Building:** Emphasize the importance of building relationships slowly and intentionally. By taking the time to gradually get to know someone, you can create a solid foundation of trust and understanding, reducing the risk of misunderstandings and emotional hurt.
- **Cautious Closeness Assessment:** Recognize that closeness in certain relationships is not always worth the potential risks. Carefully assess whether the rewards of a deeper relationship outweigh the fears and vulnerabilities involved. If the balance tips towards more harm than good, it may be wise to maintain a healthy distance, not only in love but also in business, friendships, and more.

Summary:

The Hedgehogs' Dilemma encapsulates the paradox of human intimacy, illustrating the fine line between closeness and the potential for emotional hurt. By understanding the principles outlined in this chapter, you can navigate your relationships with greater empathy and awareness, fostering deeper, more meaningful connections while mitigating the risks of emotional harm.

Chapter 37: The Power of Asking Interactive Chapter 5

"You miss 100% of the shots you don't take."

– Wayne Gretzky

Graphical Representation:

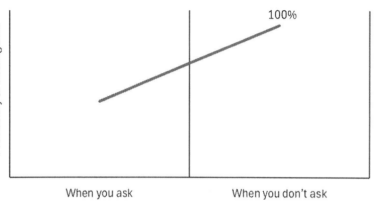

Reflective Exercise:

Examine the graph showing the transition from the potential of 'Asking' to the impossibility of 'Not Asking.' Consider these thoughts:
- Reflect on a moment when fear of rejection stopped you from asking for something. What could have changed if you had asked?
- Reflect on a successful outcome that stemmed from a simple question you had the courage to ask.

Closing Thought:

Don't let the fear of hearing 'no' hold you back. If you never ask, the answer will always be no. If you don't try, you'll never discover what could have been. Are you really afraid of the minor sting that a 'no' can bring? This hesitation acts as the gateway to the Hedgehog's Dilemma: a small emotional discomfort that can prevent us from taking the first step. This principle isn't limited to personal relationships – it extends to decision-making, business, risk-taking, and beyond. Engage boldly, and don't let the small discomfort of a 'no' keep you from discovering the 'yes' that could change everything.

Part 6
The Productivity Graphs

"Focus on being productive instead of busy."

– Tim Ferriss

Welcome to the realm of productivity graphs, where we'll explore the strategies and insights that lead to effective management and personal growth. In this part, we'll uncover the keys to unlocking your potential and achieving success in all facets of life. As we journey through these graphs, you'll discover how to optimize your time, energy, and resources, propelling you toward your goals with newfound efficiency and effectiveness.

Chapter 38: Parkinson's Law

"Work expands so as to fill the time available for its completion."

– Cyril Northcote Parkinson

Principle Introduction:

Parkinson's Law states that the amount of work required adjusts to fill the entire time available for its completion. It highlights our tendency to stretch tasks to match their deadlines, even if they could be finished earlier, leading to less efficient work habits. Understanding this principle encourages setting tighter deadlines and avoiding needless prolongation of work, thereby enhancing productivity.

Graphical Representations:

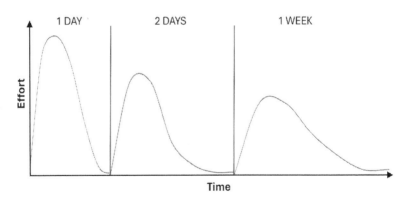

Graphical Key Points:

- Each graph represents the entire process of completing the same specific task, from start to finish. The task itself remains constant across all three scenarios.

- The time allocated for task completion varies across the graphs, with the first graph representing a 1-day timeframe, the second graph depicting a 2-day period, and the third graph illustrating a 1-week duration.
- The work expands to fill the entire time given and concludes only when the deadline is reached, regardless of the allocated duration.

Life Scenario:

Students are given three weeks to complete a project report. In the first week, instead of starting the report, they research extensively, far beyond what is needed. In the second week, they focus on perfecting the formatting rather than writing the content. By the third week, they rush to write and submit the report, which now truly requires the remainder of the time due to the prior expansion of preparatory tasks.

Wider Implications:

- **Meeting Agendas:** In corporate settings, meeting times often get filled with discussions that may not be essential. Setting a strict agenda with allocated times for each topic can prevent meetings from overrunning and ensure that only important issues are covered.
- **Travel Packing:** When packing for a trip, people often fill their suitcases to the brim, regardless of the actual necessity of all items. Setting a limit on the number of items or using a smaller suitcase can lead to more efficient packing and less unnecessary baggage.
- **Social media and Screen Time:** The amount of time spent on social media and other digital platforms

often expands to fill any available leisure time, potentially detracting from other valuable activities such as physical exercise, reading, or face-to-face social interactions. Setting deliberate limits on screen time and scheduling specific periods for digital activity can help individuals regain control over their time, leading to a more balanced and fulfilling lifestyle.

Principle Origins:

Parkinson's Law originated from an article written by Cyril Northcote Parkinson, a British historian, in "The Economist" on November 19, 1955. He drew from his observations of the British Civil Service and noted, humorously, that bureaucracies expand over time even if there is no actual increase in work. Parkinson used the example of the British Colonial Office, which grew as the British Empire declined, with the greatest number of staff present when it was folded into the Foreign Office due to a lack of colonies to administer. He attributed this growth to two factors: officials' desire to multiply subordinates (not rivals) and to make work for each other. The law was translated into many languages and became popular globally, noted for its application in various bureaucratic systems and other fields.

Analyzing the Principle:

- **Procrastination and Time Perception:** Parkinson's Law often manifests due to our natural tendency to procrastinate. When faced with a distant deadline, we perceive an abundance of time, leading to a relaxed approach. As the deadline approaches, our perception of time shifts, and we suddenly find ourselves working more efficiently. This change in time perception illustrates how our motivation and work pace are directly influenced by the looming deadline.

- **Perfectionism and Fear of Failure:** The law taps into the perfectionist tendencies and fear of failure many individuals face. With longer deadlines, there's a psychological push to make everything perfect, often going beyond what is necessary. This perfectionism isn't just about improving quality but is also a form of procrastination driven by the fear of criticism or failure. The ample time becomes a double-edged sword, encouraging overthinking and unnecessary adjustments that inflate the workload.
- **Resource Saturation:** Just as tasks tend to expand to fill allocations of time, we tend to maximize our usage of other available resources, even beyond our actual requirements. This is seen in budgetary spending, manpower, and other fields which are maximized not always out of necessity but because they are available, highlighting an inefficiency in resource allocation.

Insights to Implement in Life:

- **The Power of Limits:** Create your own, earlier deadlines for tasks to combat the natural expansion of work. This self-imposed time constraint forces prioritization, encourages quicker decision-making, and can significantly increase your productivity by preventing tasks from unnecessarily dragging on.
- **Embrace the Minimum Viable Product (MVP) Mindset:** Whether it's for work projects, personal goals, or creative endeavors, focus on achieving a

'good enough' standard that meets the requirements instead of aiming for perfection. This approach allows you to complete tasks more efficiently and allocate time to refine them later, if necessary, instead of getting bogged down in details from the start.
- **Break It Down and Time It Out:** When faced with a large, complex task, break it down into smaller, more manageable sub-tasks. Allocate specific time slots for each sub-task based on its complexity and importance. This approach not only makes the overall task less daunting but also helps you maintain focus and motivation as you progress through each sub-task. By setting clear time boundaries for each component, you can prevent the entire task from expanding indefinitely and ensure a more structured and efficient workflow.

Summary:

Parkinson's Law highlights our tendency to use up all the allotted time for a task, often leading to inefficiency. This principle can be applied across various realms of life, from education and healthcare to creative industries and urban planning, encouraging more focused and efficient work habits. When combined with Pareto's Law (Chapter 6), which suggests that 80% of results come from 20% of efforts, we find a powerful approach to productivity – by setting tighter deadlines (Parkinson's Law) and focusing on the most impactful tasks (Pareto's Law), we can optimize our efforts, reduce wasted time, and achieve more with less, leading to greater overall efficiency and effectiveness in our personal and professional lives.

Chapter 39: The Yerkes-Dodson Law

"Stress is the spice of life."

– Hans Selye

Principle Introduction:

The Yerkes-Dodson Law illustrates a crucial aspect of human performance: the relationship between stress and our ability to carry out tasks. It posits that there is a sweet spot of stress that can enhance our performance, unlike the commonly held belief that all stress is detrimental. This chapter will present how the delicate balance of stress influences our efficiency and productivity.

Graphical Representation:

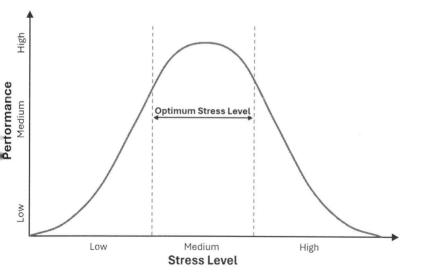

Graphical Key Points:

- **The Low-Stress Underperformance:** On the left, the graph starts with low levels of stress leading to poor performance.
- **The Optimal Stress Apex:** The peak of the curve represents the optimal stress level, where our performance is at its highest.
- **The High-Stress Decline:** Past the optimal point, the graph shows performance deteriorating as stress levels continue to increase.

Life Scenario:

Imagine a salesperson working under the pressure of a deadline. With too little stress, they may lack the drive to pursue leads aggressively. With too much stress, they might become overwhelmed and make mistakes. However, the right amount of stress can energize and motivate them to close sales effectively and efficiently.

Wider Implications:

- **Professional Environments:** understanding this law can lead to better workload management to enhance employee performance.
- **Sport Psychology:** Athletes can use the Yerkes-Dodson Law to find their optimal stress level for competition. By understanding their own stress-performance relationship, they can use techniques like visualization, breathing exercises, or music to achieve the right balance and enhance their performance.
- **Education and Learning:** Educators can apply the principles of the Yerkes-Dodson Law to create an optimal learning environment. By balancing the challenge

of the material with the exact time needed for each exercise, teachers can foster engagement and focus, leading to better learning outcomes.

Principle Origins:

In 1908, psychologists Robert M. Yerkes and John Dillingham Dodson formulated this law through their work with mice. They observed that a moderate level of electric shock could motivate mice to navigate a maze effectively, suggesting that a similar principle could apply to human behavior and performance.

Analyzing the Principle:

- **Neurological Basis:** The Yerkes-Dodson Law is rooted in the brain's response to arousal. Arousal activates the sympathetic nervous system, which prepares the body for action by increasing heart rate, blood flow, and energy levels. This heightened state can enhance cognitive and physical performance up to a point. However, excessive arousal can overload the brain's cognitive capacity, leading to decreased performance due to stress and anxiety.
- **Attentional Control:** Stress levels influence attentional control, which is crucial for performance. Moderate stress enhances the brain's ability to focus and filter out distractions, leading to better task performance. However, when stress is too high, it can disrupt attentional control, making it harder to concentrate and process information effectively, resulting in poorer performance.
- **Connection to the Flow State (Chapter 2):** The optimal level of stress in the Yerkes-Dodson Law is crucial

for entering the flow state. If stress is too low or too high, it can prevent the deep immersion and enjoyment characteristic of flow, which is the most effective mental state.

Insights to Implement in Life:

- **Maximize Effectiveness in Low-Stress Situations:** While high-stress situations can make it difficult to control the effectiveness level, low-stress environments offer a unique opportunity to enhance productivity against our tendency towards complacency. In these moments, it's important to stay alert and avoid unnecessary ineffectiveness.
- **Strategic Learning Through Progressive Task Complexity:** Begin projects with easier tasks that align with your optimal stress level, and progressively tackle more complex challenges. This method keeps stress levels optimal, boosting concentration and efficiency while keeping engagement high and staving off burnout.
- **Take Active Breaks:** If you notice your stress levels climbing too high, it's a sign that you might not be working as efficiently as possible. Take periodic breaks to reset – go for a walk, watch a short funny video, or engage in a relaxing activity to bring your stress level back down to your optimal zone.

Summary:

The Yerkes-Dodson Law offers valuable insight into the dual nature of stress, serving both as a motivator and a hindrance, depending on its level. By striving for the optimal stress point, you can achieve your highest potential in various activities, from simple to complex tasks. This law encourages us to view stress not just as a challenge to overcome, but as a potential ally in our pursuit of excellence.

Chapter 40: Life's Friction

"The greatest amount of wasted time is the time not getting started."

– Dawson Trotman

Principle Introduction:

This chapter compares the friction we encounter when starting new ventures to the frictional forces in physics. The hardest part of starting motion is the beginning, much like the initial force needed to overcome static friction is greater than the force required once things are in motion, reflecting kinetic friction.

Graphical Representation:

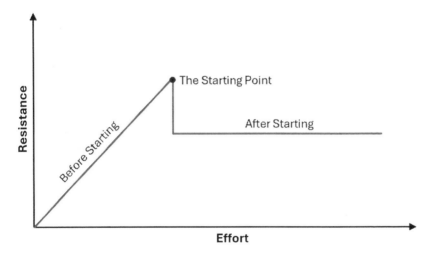

Graphical Key Points:

- **"The Uphill Start"** – The steep initial effort to overcome inertia.

- **"The Breakthrough"** – The peak point where action starts.
- **"The Steady Stride"** – An easier steady effort.

Life Scenario:

Imagine the effort it takes to start a daily running routine. The first few days feel the hardest, as you push through the mental 'static friction.' Once the habit is formed, the 'kinetic friction' of daily running feels much easier to maintain.

Wider Implications:

- **Personal Development:** Whether it's learning a new skill, adopting a healthier lifestyle, or practicing yoga, the initial effort to start these personal development activities is often the hardest and once started, it's easier to make them part of a routine.
- **Financial Management:** Starting a savings plan or investing for the future can be daunting at first. However, once the initial step is taken, managing finances becomes a more manageable and routine part of life.
- **Technology Adoption:** Introducing new technologies in organizations or communities often faces resistance at first, but once adopted, it can lead to smoother operations.

Principle Origins:

The idea is rooted in the fundamental frictional forces in physics, a topic we shall not explore in great depth for our mutual benefit (if you're curious, this is the equation: $\mu_k < \mu_s$). In essence, this principle indicates that starting from a complete stop requires overcoming the highest resistance. Once motion is initiated, the effort required to maintain it is less than before. This mirrors a familiar aspect of life: taking the first step is often the most challenging part.

Analyzing the Principle:

- **Psychological Inertia:** Just as objects resist changes in their state of motion, humans resist changes in their behavior or habits. This resistance is rooted in our brain's preference for familiar patterns and the comfort of routine.
- **Habit Formation:** The formation of habits is a crucial mechanism in reducing the mental effort required to continue a task. As actions become routine, they require less conscious thought, effectively lowering the 'mental friction' that hinders progress. This process is similar to how a well-oiled machine operates more smoothly over time.
- **Self-Efficacy and Momentum:** The graph's initial slope, representing the uphill start, is influenced by an individual's self-efficacy, or the belief in their ability to execute actions and achieve goals. Higher self-efficacy leads to a smoother start, as individuals are more confident in their ability to succeed. In addition, the representation of momentum in the graph is oversimplified. In reality, maintaining momentum over time is affected by changing circumstances, evolving goals, and external pressures. These factors can make sustaining effort either easier or more challenging, highlighting the dynamic nature of the journey beyond the initial inertia.

Insights to Implement in Life:

- **Start with an Easy First Step:** To overcome the initial resistance, begin with a simple, manageable task. Open a Word document for your project, set an alarm for tomorrow's practice, prepare your workspace, or hook a specific time with friends. These easy first steps can reduce the mental barrier of starting.
- **Consistency is Key:** Once you've started, don't stop, maintaining momentum is crucial. Remember, it's easier to keep going than to start from scratch each time. In addition, consistent efforts help solidify habits and make the journey smoother by reducing the friction of the momentum itself.
- **Reward Systems:** Implementing a reward system can significantly reduce the mental friction associated with starting a new task. By associating a positive outcome with the completion of a task, the brain is more inclined to initiate action, overcoming the initial resistance. For example, if you need to start a crucial report at work, you might promise yourself lunch at your favorite restaurant once you've finished the first 3 pages.

Summary:

This chapter addresses the metaphorical 'friction' faced when starting any new journey. It reassures us that while the first step may be the hardest, it's the most crucial, and the journey will become easier as we move forward, much like overcoming static friction to benefit from kinetic friction's ease.

Chapter 41: The Over-Justification Effect

"We often lose interest in things when we are rewarded for doing them."

Principle Introduction:

The Over-justification Effect describes how external rewards can affect intrinsic motivation to engage in a behavior or activity. This psychological principle suggests that when an external incentive is given to perform an activity that is already internally rewarding, the intrinsic interest may decrease.

Graphical Representation:

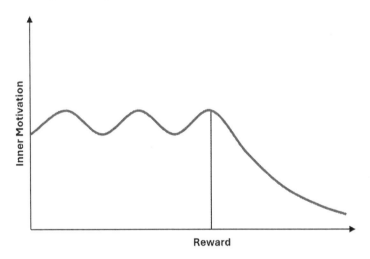

Graphical Key Points:

- The graph displays a line that represents inner motivation, which remains relatively stable at first.

- There is a point where a reward is introduced.
- After the reward is given, intrinsic motivation starts to decrease, suggesting that the reward has a lasting negative impact on the person's internal drive.

Life Scenario:

Imagine a company that introduces a bonus system for employees who complete their tasks ahead of schedule. While this might initially boost productivity, employees who previously took pride in their work might begin to focus only on the tasks that earn them bonuses, neglecting other important aspects of their job. Over time, their intrinsic motivation to excel in their role could diminish, as their primary drive becomes the pursuit of bonuses rather than personal or professional growth.

Wider Implications:

- **In Education:** Understanding the negative impact of rewards on student motivation.
- **In the Workplace:** Balancing intrinsic and extrinsic motivators for employee engagement.
- **In Parenting:** Nurturing children's intrinsic interests without over-relying on external rewards.

Principle Origins:

The over-justification effect was first demonstrated in a seminal experiment conducted by psychologist Edward Deci in 1971. Deci was curious about how external rewards affect intrinsic motivation. He recruited college students who already had a baseline interest in solving puzzles, suggesting intrinsic motivation. The students participated in three puzzle-solving sessions.

In the first session, all solved puzzles without any reward. In the second session, one group was offered money to solve puzzles, while a control group received no incentive. Deci found that students who had expected monetary rewards showed less interest and spent less time solving puzzles in a later session without rewards, compared to the control group. This suggested that the external reward undermined their initial intrinsic motivation for the activity. Deci's experiment provided empirical evidence that extrinsic rewards can decrease intrinsic motivation, laying the foundation for the over-justification effect theory.

Analyzing the Principle:

- **Shift of Focus:** When rewards are introduced, the focus shifts from the enjoyment of the activity to the outcome or reward, which can make the activity itself feel less enjoyable.
- **Perceived Over-Control:** Rewards can create a sense of being controlled by external factors, which can lead to resistance and a decrease in natural interest in the activity.
- **Diminished Autonomy:** Receiving rewards for an activity can make it feel less like a choice and more like an obligation, reducing the personal satisfaction one gets from doing it.

Insights to Implement in Life:

- **Balance Rewards and Recognition:** In any rewarding system, whether in personal, educational, or professional settings, strive for a balance between extrin-

sic rewards and intrinsic motivation. Use rewards as a form of recognition without making them the primary focus.
- **Monitor Reward Impact on Motivation:** Consistently review the effect that external rewards, like bonuses or commendations, have on the inherent motivation of you or your team. Consider how motivation levels might shift in the absence of such incentives.
- **Use Rewards When Necessary:** Sometimes, giving rewards is necessary to boost motivation. Don't completely avoid using them, only be mindful not to overdo it. Use rewards as a tool to enhance motivation without relying on them too heavily.

Summary:

This chapter explored the Over-justification Effect, shedding light on the delicate balance between intrinsic and extrinsic motivators. Understanding this principle is crucial in various fields, from education and parenting to organizational behavior, in order to nurture genuine interest and engagement.

Chapter 42: The Zeigarnik Effect

"Our minds quickly forget finished tasks. However, they are programmed to continually interrupt us with reminders of unfinished tasks."

— Bluma Zeigarnik

Principle Introduction:

The Zeigarnik Effect is a psychological phenomenon where uncompleted or interrupted tasks are remembered better than completed ones. This principle highlights our brain's focus on unfinished tasks, creating a mental tension that seeks resolution.

Graphical Representation:

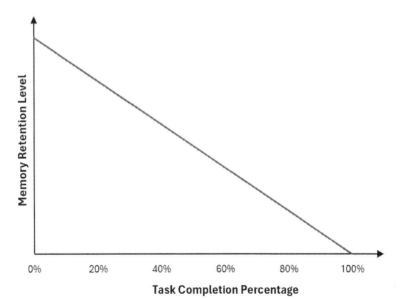

Graphical Key Points:

- Memory retention levels are at their maximum when a task is at 0% completion, implying that uninitiated tasks are most prominent in memory.
- There is a negative correlation between the degree of task completion and memory retention – as task completion progresses, memory retention consistently declines.
- Upon reaching 100% completion, memory retention finally reaches zero, indicating that completed tasks are least likely to be retained in memory.

Life Scenario:

You start reading a book for a university report next week but get interrupted halfway through. In the following days, you find yourself constantly thinking about needing to finish it while dealing with a nagging tension as you try not to forget it and struggle to fully focus on other assignments until you complete it.

Wider Implications:

- **Creative Writing:** Writers can use the Zeigarnik effect to build suspense in stories by leaving chapters on cliffhangers.
- **Gaming:** Video games often employ the Zeigarnik effect, using unfinished quests or levels to keep players engaged.
- **Culinary Arts:** Chefs can structure a meal experience by leaving diners anticipating the next course, enhancing the overall dining experience.

Principle Origins:

Bluma Zeigarnik discovered what we now know as the Zeigarnik Effect in 1927, following her professor Kurt Lewin's curiosity about waiters' memory for unpaid orders. Her studies showed better recall for interrupted tasks, suggesting that the brain maintains better memory for incomplete tasks.

Analyzing the Principle:

- **Cognitive Tension:** Incomplete tasks create a tension in our minds due to the fear of forgetting them. This tension acts as a mental reminder, pushing us to finish what we've started to relieve the unease.
- **Finished vs. Unfinished Tasks:** Unfinished tasks are continuously processed in the background, keeping them active in our memory, which contrasts with the processing of completed tasks that are archived and become less accessible.
- **The Forgetting Curve (Chapter 11):** The Zeigarnik Effect suggests that incomplete tasks are remembered well even after longer periods, which directly counters the typical pattern of the Forgetting Curve. While the Forgetting Curve indicates that memories fade over time, the Zeigarnik Effect implies that unfinished tasks resist this fading process, remaining more prominent in our memory.

Insights to Implement in Life:

- **The 'Two-Minute Rule':** Immediately act on tasks that you can complete in two minutes or less. Completing these tasks right away can reduce mental clutter and free up cognitive resources for more complex

projects, aligning with the Zeigarnik effect by preventing the accumulation of too many 'open loops' in your mind.
- **Manage Mental Clutter with a 'Parking Lot':** To avoid the mental clutter of multiple unfinished tasks, create a 'parking lot' list where you jot down tasks you've started but can't complete immediately. This helps externalize the cognitive tension, allowing you to focus on the task at hand while knowing you have a plan to revisit the unfinished ones later. This technique can be particularly useful in managing creative endeavors, personal learning goals, or even planning social events.
- **Mindful Reflections on Unfinished Business:** Use the Zeigarnik effect as a cue for personal reflection. Unfinished business in your personal life, such as unresolved conflicts or unspoken words, can weigh heavily on your mind. By addressing these issues directly, you can find closure and reduce the mental load they impose, leading to a more peaceful state of mind.

Summary:

This chapter explored the Zeigarnik effect from various perspectives, including its psychological basis, practical applications, and implications for productivity and mental health. By understanding and applying this principle, individuals can enhance memory retention, manage tasks with more focus, and potentially improve mental well-being.

Chapter 43: The Red Queen Hypothesis

"It takes all the running you can do, to keep in the same place."

— Lewis Carroll, "Through the Looking-Glass"

Principle Introduction:

The Red Queen hypothesis, derived from Lewis Carroll's "Through the Looking-Glass," is a metaphor for the constant struggle of organisms to adapt and evolve in response to their ever-changing environment. This principle is not only prevalent in biological evolution but also in various aspects of human society and technology.

Graphical Representation:

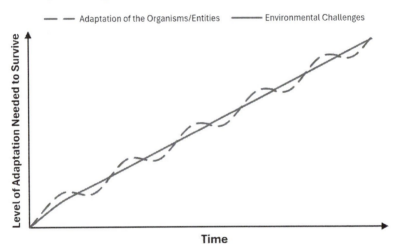

Graphical Key Points:

- **Initial Adaptation:** The start shows organisms or entities beginning their journey of adaptation. There's a

steady upward trend in adaptation, reflecting continuous improvement.
- **Environmental Challenges:** Alongside adaptation, environmental challenges also rise, suggesting a parallel struggle.
- **Fluctuations in Progress:** The graph shows fluctuations in adaptation progress, indicating the dynamic nature of evolutionary competition.

Life Scenario:

In the business world, companies constantly innovate to stay competitive. For instance, in the smartphone industry, as one company introduces a new technology, others quickly follow suit, leading to a continuous cycle of innovation where no single company maintains a lasting advantage.

Wider Implications:

- **Educational Evolution:** The ever-changing demands of the job market and advancements in technology require continuous updates to educational curricula. The Red Queen Hypothesis highlights the necessity for educational institutions to adapt their programs and teaching methods to prepare students for the future, ensuring they remain relevant and effective in equipping learners with the skills needed for success.
- **Environmental Policies:** As the challenges of climate change evolve, so must our environmental policies. The Red Queen Hypothesis underscores the need for dynamic adaptation in our strategies to combat environmental threats. Policymakers and environmentalists must stay one step ahead, constantly revising and

updating policies to effectively address the changing landscape of ecological challenges.
- **Corporate Competition:** In the business world, companies are in a constant battle to outperform their competitors. The Red Queen Hypothesis is evident as businesses must continually innovate, improve their products and services, and adapt to market changes to stay ahead. This relentless drive for innovation ensures that companies remain competitive and relevant in an ever-evolving market landscape.

Principle Origins:

The Red Queen Hypothesis, introduced by biologist Leigh Van Valen in 1973, draws its name from the Red Queen's race in Lewis Carroll's novel "Through the Looking-Glass," where the Red Queen tells Alice that in her land, "it takes all the running you can do, to keep in the same place." Van Valen used this metaphor to describe an evolutionary hypothesis, emphasizing how species must continuously adapt to survive against ever-evolving competitors.

For example: Consider the ongoing evolutionary arms race between predators and their prey. For instance, cheetahs and gazelles are locked in a constant battle for survival. As cheetahs evolve to become faster, gazelles must also evolve to increase their speed and agility. This perpetual cycle of adaptation ensures that neither species can afford to become complacent, as any decrease in their ability to adapt could lead to their extinction.

Analyzing the Principle:

- **Survival of the Fittest:** In nature, organisms are engaged in a continuous struggle for survival and

reproduction. This competition drives species to adapt and evolve to outcompete others for limited resources, mates, and to avoid predation. The Red Queen Hypothesis highlights this relentless race, where staying ahead is crucial for survival.
- **Ecological Interactions:** The complex web of ecological interactions, such as predator-prey relationships, competition for resources, and symbiotic relationships, creates a dynamic environment where species must continuously adapt to the actions of others. These interactions can change rapidly, forcing species to evolve to maintain their ecological niches.
- **Cultural Evolution:** The Red Queen Hypothesis can be extended to human cultural evolution, where societies are in a constant race to adapt to technological advancements, shifting social norms, and global challenges. As one culture develops a new technology or ideology, others must adapt to keep up with the pace, leading to a continuous cycle of innovation and change. This dynamic drives the rapid evolution of cultural practices, beliefs, and institutions, reflecting the Red Queen's principle of needing to run just to stay in the same place in the context of human civilization.

Insights to Implement in Life:

- **Embrace Lifelong Learning and Adaptation:** In a world where change is the only constant, embracing lifelong learning and adaptation is essential for staying relevant and thriving. This means constantly seeking new knowledge, skills, and experiences to keep pace with the evolving landscape of your field or industry. By adopting a mindset of continuous growth, you can

navigate the challenges of change with confidence and seize opportunities that come your way.
- **Anticipate Change:** Rather than merely reacting to changes as they occur, it's crucial to anticipate and prepare for them proactively. This proactive approach allows you to stay ahead in any competitive environment, whether it's in your career, business, or personal life. By forecasting future trends and planning accordingly, you can position yourself to capitalize on emerging opportunities and mitigate potential risks.
- **Balance Innovation with Sustainability:** While embracing constant adaptation and innovation is crucial for progress, it's equally important to ensure that these changes do not undermine what you've built so far. This means carefully considering the long-term implications of your actions and striving for a balance that preserves your core values, achievements, and resources.

Summary:

The Red Queen hypothesis encapsulates the relentless race of adaptation and evolution in various spheres of life. From biological ecosystems to corporate landscapes, this principle highlights the necessity of continuous improvement and innovation to maintain one's position in a constantly changing environment.

Chapter 44: The Incremental Triumphs Framework

"Great things are not done by impulse, but by a series of small things brought together."

– Vincent Van Gogh

Principle Introduction:

In a world that often celebrates only grand victories, the Incremental Triumphs Framework shifts focus to the cumulative power of small wins. Each minor success is a step on the staircase to greatness, reinforcing motivation and fostering a sense of progress that is critical for sustained achievement and personal well-being.

Graphical Representation:

Graphical Key Points:

- **Small Wins:** The graph presents a series of upward steps, each one indicating a small win.

- **Sustained Gains:** These small wins show consistent progress towards a larger goal over time.
- **Major Triumph:** The meaningful achievement maintained after the accumulation of small wins.

Life Scenario:

A novice runner begins training with short distances, celebrating each additional kilometer achieved. Over months, these increments lead to his first marathon completion, illustrating the accumulative power of small victories.

Wider Implications:

- **Personal Finance Management:** By applying the Incremental Triumphs Framework to finances, individuals can set small, achievable savings goals. For example, saving an extra $50 each month can lead to a substantial emergency fund over time.
- **Personal Relationships:** In relationships, small wins can take the form of daily acts of kindness, active listening, or regular communication. These actions, over time, can strengthen the bond between individuals and foster a deeper sense of connection and trust.
- **Environmental Conservation:** In the realm of environmental conservation, small wins can manifest as daily actions like using a reusable water bottle, carpooling, or planting a garden. These actions, while seemingly minor, collectively contribute to a larger positive impact on the planet.

Principle Origins:

In the late 1990s and early 2000s, psychologists Karl Weick and Kathleen Sutcliffe studied how teams in high-pressure environments like firefighting crews and hospital ERs achieved success. Through observations and interviews, they found that breaking down complex goals into "small wins" provided frequent progress reinforcement, sustaining motivation and fostering a sense of control.

Analyzing the Principle:

- **Dopamine Release:** Each small win triggers the brain's reward system, releasing dopamine and reinforcing the behavior that led to the win.
- **Reduced Overwhelm:** Breaking down tasks into smaller goals makes challenges seem more manageable, reducing anxiety and procrastination.
- **The Snowball Effect:** The positive emotions stemming from small wins serve as reinforcement, encouraging a continued effort that gains momentum, ultimately leading to substantial change.

Insights to Implement in Life:

- **Micro-Goal Milestones:** Establishing micro-goals that are steps toward your ultimate objective is crucial. This strategy allows for frequent assessment and course correction, ensuring that you are always on the right path. By breaking down the journey into smaller, more manageable segments, you can maintain a sense of momentum and clarity, making the overall goal seem less daunting and more achievable.
- **Celebrate Progress:** It's important to take time to celebrate each small victory along the way. Acknowledging and celebrating progress, no matter how minor, helps maintain motivation and focus. These celebrations can

serve as reminders of how far you've come and can provide the encouragement needed to continue pushing forward.
- **Patience in Plateaus:** Recognizing and accepting that plateaus are a natural part of the process is vital. There will be times when significant progress isn't immediately apparent, but maintaining efforts during these periods is crucial. Patience during these times can prevent discouragement and ensure that you stay committed to your long-term goals, even when the path forward seems slow.

Summary:

The Incremental Triumphs Framework invites you to embrace the compound effect of small wins and rethink your definition of success. It's a reminder that the journey to your most significant achievements is built on a foundation of many small, easily overlooked victories. Each step you take, no matter how small, is a crucial piece of the puzzle, moving you closer to your goals.

Chapter 45: The Reflection Ripple Effect Interactive Chapter 6

"We do not learn from experience... we learn from reflecting on experience."

– John Dewey

Graphical Representation:

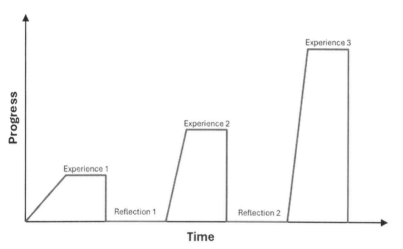

Reflective Exercise:

Look at the graph's ascents and plateaus and see them as symbols of your own progress and pauses for contemplation. Ask yourself:
- When was the last time you took a genuine pause after an eventful experience to reflect on what transpired?
- Can you think of a moment when reflection altered the course of your actions, perhaps transforming a setback into a stepping stone?

Closing Thought:

Reflection serves as a quiet guide for productivity, turning experiences into valuable lessons that shape a wiser path forward. It's the tool that transforms the past into a foundation for future growth.

Part 7
The Advanced Graphs

"To understand is to perceive patterns."

– Isaiah Berlin

Step into the realm of advanced graphs, where we'll explore the mysteries and complexities of life that lie beyond the surface. This part challenges your understanding and invites deep reflection on the intricate patterns and principles that govern our existence. As we delve into these sophisticated concepts, you'll be equipped to view life through a new lens, uncovering insights and wisdom that illuminate the path to a deeper comprehension of the world around us.

Chapter 46: Life's 3 Ages

"Growing old is mandatory, but growing up is optional."

– Walt Disney

Principle Introduction:

We often consider age as the number of candles on our birthday cake, but this perspective is merely the tip of the iceberg. This chapter peels back the layers, revealing a triad of factors that truly define what age means. Welcome to the crossroads of the chronological, biological, and emotional age – where the years we've lived are just the beginning of the story.

Graphical Representation:

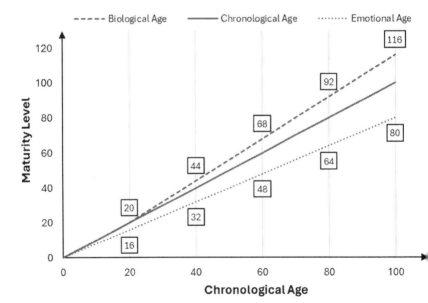

Graphical Key Points:

- This is a specific graph illustrating this example: a person who exhibits some **childlike tendencies** for his age and began **smoking at the age of 20**.
- **Emotional Age (dotted line):** Consistently remains below Chronological age, indicating a steady level of emotional underdevelopment relative to chronological time. Highlights a consistent lag in emotional maturity.
- **Biological Age (dashed line):** This line represents a deviation from Chronological age, starting at age 20. In this example, the case involves smoking from age 20 onwards. However, accelerations in the Biological Age can also result from other unhealthy lifestyle choices, including lack of exercise, poor nutrition, and more.

Life Scenario:

- **Biological Age:** A 50-year-old marathon runner may have a biological age that is younger than their chronological age due to their excellent physical condition and healthy lifestyle choices.
- **Emotional Age:** A 25-year-old entrepreneur may display an emotional age that surpasses their chronological age, showcasing maturity and emotional intelligence in navigating the challenges of starting a business.

Wider Implications:

- **Healthcare:** Tailoring treatments to an individual's biological age rather than their chronological age for more effective care.
- **Education:** Addressing the emotional maturity of students to inform appropriate pedagogical approaches.

- **Workplace:** Understanding the emotional age of employees to enhance team dynamics and leadership strategies.

Principle Origins:

The concepts of chronological, biological, and emotional age have evolved over time through various studies and theoretical developments, without a single point of origin. Studies in the late 20th and early 21st centuries have focused on biomarkers and physiological measures to assess biological aging. Emotional age is explored within the context of lifespan development and psychological theories. The differentiation between these aspects of age is recognized in fields such as gerontology, psychology, and medicine.

Analyzing the Principle:

- **Chronological Age:** This is the most straightforward measure, representing the number of years since birth.
- **Biological Age:** This takes into account the physical condition of the body and can vary significantly from chronological age based on lifestyle choices, genetics, and environmental factors. It's a more accurate indicator of health and longevity.
- **Emotional Age:** This reflects an individual's emotional maturity and development. It's influenced by experiences, relationships, and personal growth. A mismatch between emotional and chronological age can lead to challenges in coping with life's demands.

Insights to Implement in Life:

- **Understand Society:** The three ages concept enables you to empathize with people in society who may have different emotional ages. This empathy promotes better understanding and more harmonious interactions with diverse individuals.
- **Resist Biological Aging:** Embrace a lifestyle that promotes physical wellness and vitality, actively challenging the natural progression of biological aging to maintain a youthful vigor.
- **Foster Emotional Growth:** Emotional maturity doesn't develop automatically with age. It requires active engagement, stepping beyond comfort zones, and a willingness to learn from life's experiences to cultivate emotional intelligence and resilience.

Summary:

The concept of Life's 3 ages offers a new lens for viewing aging, emphasizing chronological, biological, and emotional dimensions. Understanding this concept promotes empathy and harmonious interactions in society. I suggest you slow down your biological aging through healthy choices, but when navigating emotional youth, consider its pros and cons and decide for yourself the best approach.

Chapter 47: The Law of Truly Large Numbers

"The paradoxical conclusion is that it would be very unlikely for unlikely events not to occur."

– John Allen Paulos

Principle Introduction:

The Law of Truly Large Numbers states that with a large enough number of opportunities, every event that can happen, will happen. This chapter also relates to Littlewood's Law, which suggests we pass by unnoticed 'miracles' regularly, and the Infinite Monkey Theorem, portraying the inevitability of chance given enough time.

Graphical Representation:

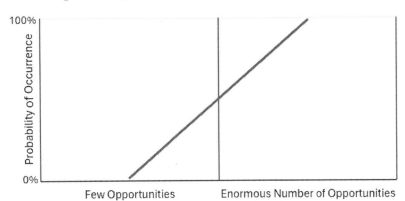

Graphical Key Points:

- The curve starts near zero, indicating a low probability of occurrence with few opportunities.
- With increasing opportunities, rare events eventually become almost certain, ultimately reaching a 100% probability of occurrence.
- I chose to use general terms like 'few' and 'enormous' instead of specific numbers because the exact figures can vary depending on the situation. It's important to focus on the general pattern that the likelihood increases with more opportunities, rather than fixating on precise numbers.

Life Scenario:

Everyday coincidences, like thinking of a friend just as they call, can seem miraculous but are statistically predictable after understanding the Law of Truly Large Numbers.

Wider Implications:

- **Infinite Monkey Theorem:** This theorem posits that a monkey hitting keys at random on a typewriter for an infinite amount of time could eventually type a complete work, such as Shakespeare's "Hamlet."
- **Littlewood's Law:** Littlewood's Law complements the law by proving mathematically that individuals can encounter miraculous events about once a month given the vast number of opportunities present in daily life.
- **Financial Planning:** Discerning between genuine investment patterns and randomness.

Principle Origins:

John Allen Paulos introduced the Law of Truly Large Numbers in his 1988 book "Innumeracy: Mathematical Illiteracy and its Consequences." He aimed to illustrate how a lack of understanding of numbers and probability can lead to a variety of misinterpretations and erroneous beliefs in society. By emphasizing the vast difference between our intuitions and the realities of numerical concepts, Paulos explained phenomena such as the overestimation of rare events and the underestimation of coincidences. The book, encouraged a more quantitative view of the world, tackling topics from pseudoscience to public policy through engaging anecdotes and scenarios.

Analyzing the Principle:

- **Probability Blindness:** Humans often navigate life without actively tracking the probability of events, which leads to a lack of awareness about the sheer number of opportunities encountered. This unawareness obscures the realization of how "enormous" the cumulative chances for various outcomes are. Over time, this contributes to surprise or disbelief when unlikely events do occur, despite them being statistically predictable within the vast landscape of chance woven through daily life.
- **Emotional Amplification:** Rare and coincidental events often involve high emotions, which can skew our perception of their frequency even if we track it. Emotional experiences create strong memories, which can lead us to overestimate the likelihood of such events recurring.
- **Pattern Recognition Bias:** Humans are wired to recognize patterns for survival. This instinct can misfire,

causing us to detect patterns in random data, such as seeing meaningful connections in large numbers of unrelated events.

Insights to Implement in Life:

- **Critical Numeracy:** Develop a better understanding of probability and statistics. This isn't just for mathematicians, it's a practical skill for making informed decisions in everyday life, from understanding health risks to interpreting news reports.
- **Mindful Skepticism:** Approach extraordinary claims and coincidences with curiosity but also skepticism. Learn to ask for the statistical likelihood of such events to differentiate between truly rare phenomena and expected outcomes of chance.
- **Balanced Risk Assessment:** Use a rational approach to assess risks in life, not just the ones that make headlines or play on your emotions. This means focusing on actual probabilities to guide your actions, like investing in health insurance rather than only playing the lottery.

Summary:

By discovering the Law of Truly Large Numbers, we learn to navigate through life with a more realistic understanding of probability, enhancing our decision-making and demystifying the 'miracles' of everyday life.

Chapter 48: The Wisdom of Crowds

"Sometimes, the many are smarter than the few."

Principle Introduction:

The wisdom of the crowd principle suggests that large groups of people are collectively smarter than individual experts when it comes to problem-solving, decision-making, innovating, and predicting. This principle hinges on the diversity of opinions and decentralization, whereby individual biases and errors cancel each other out, leaving the most accurate answer.

Graphical Representation:

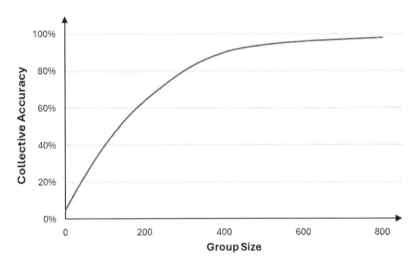

Graphical Key Points:

- The graph measures the group's collective response, reflecting the average precision of their answers.

- A sharp rise at the start shows that accuracy improves quickly with the addition of more members to the group.
- As the curve flattens out, it shows that the group maintains a high accuracy rate that nears perfection with more participants.

Life Scenario:

Predicting Winners in Sporting Events – a large group's aggregated predictions on game outcomes often surpass the accuracy of professional bookmakers.

Wider Implications:

- **Estimating Quantities:** A crowd's average estimation for items in a jar often astonishingly aligns with the actual count, showcasing the accuracy of collective judgment.
- **Market Predictions:** Crowd wisdom adeptly forecasts market fluctuations and consumer patterns, outperforming solitary expert analyses.
- **Public Policy:** Public opinion collectively guides effective policy decisions, embodying democratic principles.

Principle Origins:

The concept was popularized by James Surowiecki in his book 'The Wisdom of Crowds,' but it dates back to 1907 when Francis Galton observed the phenomenon at a country fair. Galton asked 787 individuals to guess the weight of an ox, and this included guesses from both experts, such as butchers and farmers, as well as non-experts like clerks. The crowd's average guess was nearly perfect at 1,197 pounds, compared to the actual weight of 1,198 pounds.

Analyzing the Principle:

- **Collective Expertise:** In a crowd, every individual contributes their own slice of expertise, which when pooled together, spans a broader spectrum of knowledge than any single expert could provide. This amalgamation of diverse skills and experiences can lead to a richer and more comprehensive understanding of issues.
- **Optimal Conditions:** The wisdom of crowds thrives where diverse individuals independently share ideas without bias or pressure. An ideal space might be online, allowing anonymous contributions, or a well-facilitated real-life setting ensuring equal voice. Such environments are key to unleashing the group's power for accurate predictions and innovative solutions.
- **The Law of Diminishing Returns (Chapter 7):** The Wisdom of Crowds exemplifies the Law of Diminishing Returns. In a group, decision-making accuracy continues to improve as more independent viewpoints are added, even though each new participant contributes slightly less value than the previous one.

Insights to Implement in Life:

- **Diversity in Collaboration:** Invite varied viewpoints in team projects to tap into the collective wisdom, enriching solutions with a spectrum of insights that individually might be overlooked.
- **Leveraging Technology:** Utilize digital platforms for decision-making, employing methods like anonymous voting and collective averaging to pool insights from a broad audience.

- **Caution in Application:** While the collective wisdom of crowds can be strikingly accurate in some contexts, it's crucial to discern where it applies. Crowdsourcing decisions in complex or highly specialized areas, such as medical treatments, without expert guidance could lead to misinformed choices and harmful outcomes. It's important to balance crowd input with professional expertise to avoid the pitfalls of mass judgments in sensitive or critical scenarios.

Summary:

The Wisdom of Crowds principle illuminates the power of collective intelligence and its potential to surpass individual expertise. By understanding and structuring environments to capitalize on this phenomenon, we can make more informed decisions and foster innovation across various fields.

Chapter 49: The Flynn Effect

"The undisputed fact of the Flynn effect demonstrates that human beings are capable of getting smarter, that intelligence is not determined simply by DNA."

– Rahul Jandial

Principle Introduction:

The Flynn Effect represents a fascinating and counterintuitive trend observed over the 20th century: A consistent and significant increase in IQ scores across generations worldwide. This chapter delves into the causes and implications of this phenomenon, exploring how societal changes, education, and environmental factors contribute to the global rise in cognitive abilities.

Graphical Representation:

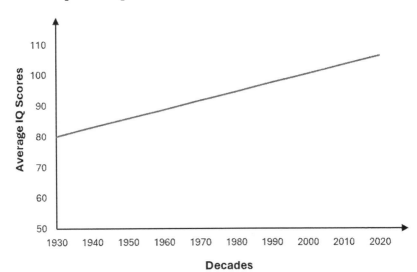

Graphical Key Points:

- The graph begins with an estimated average IQ score of 80 for the 1930s, based on the average IQ in the United States in 1932.
- A meta-analysis found a mean increase of approximately 2.31 standard score points per decade since 1951, with an estimated increase of about 2.93 points per decade overall.
- The specific scores and the rate of IQ increase can differ among various studies and populations. This graph does not combine data from all scientific studies but serves as a hypothetical representation, assuming that the rate of increase in IQ results remains constant in the present day.

Life Scenario:

In comparison to previous generations, the 20th century witnessed an unmatched surge in technological progress. With innovations like the internet, computers, AI and the birth of space exploration, this era showcased the direct link between increasing cognitive abilities in generations and the rapid development of technology.

Wider Implications:

- **Juvenoia:** The term was coined by sociologist David Finkelhor in 2010 as a blend of the words "juvenile" and "paranoia." It describes the tendency of older adults to view the younger generation as worse or less wise than previous generations, even when the evidence does not support this view. This phenomenon can lead to strained family dynamics and overprotective parenting approaches, which may inhibit children's

exploration and development in a world that appears to be advancing positively compared to previous decades.
- **Global Development:** The Flynn Effect is one of the best indicators of global development, as improvements in education, healthcare, and living conditions are reflected in rising IQ scores, suggesting progress in human capital across nations.
- **Impact on Social Dynamics:** As cognitive abilities increase, social dynamics may shift. Higher cognitive skills can lead to more complex social interactions and a greater capacity for understanding diverse perspectives and cultures, which can enhance empathy and cooperation worldwide.

Principle Origins:

James R. Flynn, a New Zealand intelligence researcher, first identified this trend, leading to its naming as the Flynn Effect. His analysis of IQ test scores over time revealed a consistent upward trajectory, prompting a reevaluation of intelligence measures and their implications for society.

Analyzing the Principle:

- **Continuous Learning World:** The continuous learning world we live in is the key factor driving improvements in various fields. Ongoing research and education lead to advancements in medical treatments and technologies. In education, the adoption of innovative teaching methods and digital learning tools enhances learning outcomes. Other fields, such as engineering, environmental science, and information technol-

ogy, also benefit from the constant accumulation and application of new knowledge, leading to progress and innovation.
- **Digital Age Impact:** Early exposure to worldwide data using advanced digital tools stimulates spatial and logical skills, reinforcing the Flynn Effect in the context of technology.
- **Nutritional and Educational Improvements:** The Flynn Effect is also attributed to enhanced nutrition and increased access to education, which together contribute to better brain development and exposure to complex cognitive tasks, enhancing overall cognitive abilities.

Insights to Implement in Life:

- **Cultivate Intergenerational Empathy:** Foster an understanding of different generational perspectives and experiences. Engage in dialogues that bridge generational divides, promoting mutual respect and shared learning. Embrace the openness of younger generations to innovative ideas, as one of these ideas could be beneficial to you.
- **Embrace Innovative Changes as Growth:** View changes in education, habits, culture, and technologies not as threats but as opportunities for growth. Reflect on how these changes can enhance your life and the lives of those around you, fostering a mindset of adaptability and openness.
- **Balance Protection and Exploration:** While it's natural to want to protect yourself and your loved ones from potential harmful development, find a balance that allows for exploration and learning. Encourage

safe, guided exploration of new ideas and technologies, fostering a sense of curiosity and resilience.

Summary:

The Flynn Effect highlights a remarkable aspect of human development, demonstrating that intelligence is not static but evolves in response to a complex interplay of environmental, educational, and societal factors. This principle encourages a hopeful outlook on human potential, emphasizing the power of progress to elevate our collective cognitive capabilities.

Chapter 50: Dunbar's Number

"You can't have too many friends."

Principle Introduction:

Dunbar's Number posits a limit to the number of stable social relationships an individual can maintain, a figure often cited as 150. This concept explores the cognitive and social constraints that govern our social circles and suggests that while we can recognize many people, social connections are limited by our brain's capacity.

Graphical Representation:

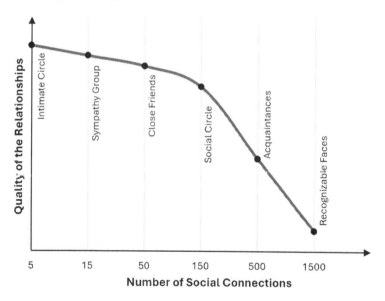

Graphical Key Points:

- **Below Dunbar's Number:** The 'Intimate Circle' and 'Sympathy Group' below Dunbar's Number represent

our closest, most supportive relationships, typically 5 to 15 individuals. These maintain the highest quality and stability of social connection.
- **Dunbar's Number:** The graph illustrates Dunbar's theory that around 150 connections is the maximum number of stable social relationships one can comfortably maintain.
- **Beyond Dunbar's Number:** Beyond 150 connections, the number of social connections continues to grow. However, these individuals fall into the categories of 'Acquaintances' and 'Recognizable Faces' – a much larger group of people we may know, but with whom our relationships are neither stable nor close.

Life Scenario:

Interaction patterns on social media platforms may reflect Dunbar's Number, where people have hundreds or thousands of 'friends' but only interact meaningfully with a fraction.

Wider Implications:

- **Community Living:** In a small community setting, residents may form close bonds within a group that naturally hovers around Dunbar's threshold.
- **Workplace Dynamics:** A corporate department where the number of employees is around 150 may exhibit a cohesive team dynamic, while larger departments might see a drop in tight-knit collaboration.
- **Customer Relationship Management (CRM):** Focus on nurturing relationships with a selected group of clients for personalized attention and loyalty.

Principle Origins:

The concept of Dunbar's Number originates from Robin Dunbar's research in the early 1990s. In his seminal 1992 paper, "Neocortex size as a constraint on group size in primates," Dunbar examined the correlation between the size of the neocortex (the part of the brain responsible for higher-order thinking) and the social group sizes of various primates. He found a consistent relationship suggesting that as the neocortex size increases, so does the ability to maintain larger social networks. Extrapolating this data to humans, Dunbar proposed that the average human brain could effectively manage about 150 stable social relationships. This theoretical limit, now known as Dunbar's Number, has since been supported by observational studies of human social groups, ranging from hunter-gatherer societies to modern social networks, which often show a clustering around this number. Dunbar's work has had significant implications for understanding the limits of human social organization and the structure of social networks.

Analyzing the Principle:

- **Cognitive Constraints:** Our brain has a limited capacity for managing the complex social demands of large networks.
- **Emotional Bandwidth:** Emotional connections require time and energy, which are naturally limited resources.
- **The Law of Diminishing Returns (Chapter 7):** Dunbar's Number aligns well with the Law of Diminishing Returns, showing that as social connections increase,

the quality of each relationship decreases due to cognitive limitations, time constraints, and emotional capacity.

Insights to Implement in Life:

- **Quality Over Quantity:** Recognize the value of deep, meaningful relationships over a wide network of shallow connections.
- **Accepting Limits:** Understand that it's normal to have a limited number of close connections, and this limit helps in forming more profound bonds.
- **Digital Interaction Awareness:** Using social media and digital communication to supplement, not replace, in-person interactions within one's Dunbar number.

Summary:

Dunbar's Number provides critical insights into the structure of human social relationships by offering a numerical limit to the stable and meaningful connections we can maintain. By understanding these social boundaries, we can more effectively manage our expectations and efforts across personal, professional, and digital interactions.

Chapter 51: The Comeback Mindset

"It's not whether you get knocked down, it's whether you get back up."

– Vince Lombardi

Principle Introduction:

The Comeback Curve illustrates the journey of persevering after a setback to achieve success. This principle is vividly embodied in Heather Dorniden's against-all-odds comeback during the 2008 Big Ten Track Championship. For a deeper appreciation of her resilience, I recommend searching online to watch the video of the race before continuing with your reading.

Graphical Representation:

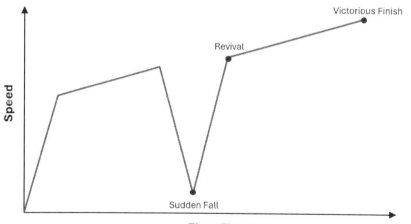

Graphical Key Points:

- **Sudden Fall:** The dramatic dip in the curve as Dorniden falls, graphically capturing her setback.
- **Remarkable Resurgence:** An exponential increase in speed as she charges ahead. Most importantly, she's running even faster than before the fall.
- **Victorious Finish:** The speed's peak is at the end when she wins the race despite the fall.

Life Scenario:

A tech startup secures an investor, then unexpectedly loses funding. Like Dorniden, they redouble their efforts and eventually thrive, achieving profitability through determination and resilience.

Wider Implications:

- **Business:** Companies that endure crises develop resilience to handle future challenges and uncertainty.
- **Relationships:** Understanding the comeback mindset helps move past conflicts or lapses in trust to rebuild bonds.
- **Sports:** Athletes can draw motivation by using failures or injuries as inspiration to bounce back stronger.

Principle Origins:

Dorniden's story offers real-life validation of psychological research on growth mindset. Her comeback illustrates that tenacity and effort can overcome adversity. Sports history contains many such tales of perseverance, but her dramatic victory is etched in lore.

Analyzing the Principle:

- **Latent Potential Activation:** Dorniden's fall triggered a latent burst of energy and speed that may have remained untapped without the setback, showing that our greatest strength often comes out when we're under pressure, even though we usually don't use it.
- **The Comeback Mindset:** More than the physical feat, Dorniden's story highlights the mental resilience we all can aspire to build. Seeing setbacks as springboards rather than roadblocks is critical for comebacks.
- **The Role of Optimism:** An optimistic outlook can act as a buffer against despair, allowing for faster recovery from setbacks and a more determined pursuit of goals.

Insights to Implement in Life:

- **Learn to Use Your Inner Reservoirs:** Engage in self-reflection to identify and tap into your hidden strengths. These reserves of power and resilience are often best accessed when challenged, but learning how to use them anytime can be a game-changer in overcoming obstacles and pursuing success.
- **It's a Setback, Not the End:** Maintain perspective, most setbacks are temporary dips on a bigger journey. Navigate them with tenacity, not catastrophe. This mindset helps you keep your eyes on long-term goals, ensuring that temporary hurdles don't derail your progress.
- **Don't Get Too Comfortable:** Setbacks are not the only obstacles; success can also lead to complacency. Celebrate your wins, but use them as motivation to aim higher. Stay focused on your next goal to keep growing and stay strong.

Summary:

Heather Dorniden's extraordinary comeback illustrates that we can achieve far more than seems possible when we rise again after setbacks. Her story is a testament to the power of passion, perseverance, and resilience.

Chapter 52: Life is All About Wins and Lessons
Interactive Chapter 7

"A life spent making mistakes is not only more honorable but more useful than a life spent doing nothing."

– George Bernard Shaw

Graphical Representation:

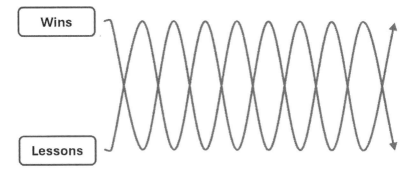

Reflective Exercise:

View the graph of two separate lines labeled 'Wins' and 'Lessons' as one of the graphical representation options of life. Ask Yourself:
- In what ways have your failures provided valuable lessons for personal growth?
- In what ways have your successes provided valuable lessons for personal growth?
- Reflect on a significant achievement. What key insights did it offer that you've applied elsewhere in your life?

Closing Thought:

Remember, every failure is a valuable lesson in disguise. Embrace these lessons as stepping stones towards your success and use them to paint a richer, more fulfilling path forward.

Graphical Independence: A Lifelong Tool

In "The Art of Thinking in Graphs," we've journeyed together to simplify life's complexities through the lens of simple graphs. Each chapter has offered a unique perspective, showing us that even the most intricate situations can be distilled into three lines. These graphs serve as a bridge, connecting abstract concepts to real-life understanding, guiding us through life's challenges with clarity and precision.

As you close this book, remember that it is much more than a collection of chapters, it is a lifelong tool. When you encounter scenarios that echo the principles we've explored, let this book be your compass. Revisit the chapters that resonate with your current challenges, and let the insights you've gained illuminate your path, helping you navigate life's twists and turns with confidence and a clearer vision.

May this book inspire you to view the world through the lens of graphs, transforming complex challenges into clear, manageable visuals. Embrace it as a guide for continuous learning, reminding you that every situation can be understood with greater clarity through the power of simple graphical representations. Here's to a future where every curve and line on a graph brings you closer to understanding the beauty and intricacy of life.

References

Chapter 1: The Dunning-Kruger Effect

Dunning, D., & Kruger, J. (1999). Unskilled and unaware of it: How difficulties in recognizing one's own incompetence lead to inflated self-assessments. Journal of Personality and Social Psychology, 77(6), 1121-1134.

Chapter 2: The Flow State

Csikszentmihalyi, M. (1990). Flow: The Psychology of Optimal Experience. Harper & Row.

Chapter 3: Loss Aversion

Kahneman, D., & Tversky, A. (1979). Prospect Theory: An Analysis of Decision under Risk. Econometrica, 47(2), 263-292.
Tversky, A., & Kahneman, D. (1991). Loss Aversion in Riskless Choice: A Reference-Dependent Model. The Quarterly Journal of Economics, 106(4), 1039-1061.

Chapter 4: The Lindy Effect

Goldman, A. (1964). Lindy's Law. The New Republic.
Mandelbrot, B. B. (1982). The Fractal Geometry of Nature. W. H. Freeman and Company.
Taleb, N. N. (2007). The Black Swan: The Impact of the Highly Improbable. Random House.
Taleb, N. N. (2012). Antifragile: Things That Gain from Disorder. Random House.

Chapter 5: The Imposter Syndrome

Clance, P. R., & Imes, S. A. (1978). The imposter phenomenon in high achieving women: Dynamics and therapeutic intervention. Psychotherapy: Theory, Research & Practice, 15(3), 241–247.

Chapter 6: The Pareto's Law (The 80/20 Principle)
Pareto, V. (1896). Cours d'économie politique. Librairie Droz.

Chapter 7: The Law of Diminishing Returns
Ricardo, D. (1817). On the Principles of Political Economy and Taxation. John Murray.

Chapter 8: Compound Interest
Bernoulli, J. (1690). Ars Conjectandi. Thurnisiorum.

Chapter 9: Cognitive Dissonance
Festinger, L. (1957). A Theory of Cognitive Dissonance. Stanford University Press.

Chapter 10: Emotional Cycle of Change
Kelley, D., & Conner, D. R. (1979). The Emotional Cycle of Change. In J. William Pfeiffer & John E. Jones (Eds.), The 1979 Annual Handbook for Group Facilitators. University Associates.

Chapter 11: The Forgetting Curve
Ebbinghaus, H. (1885). Über das Gedächtnis: Untersuchungen zur experimentellen Psychologie. Duncker & Humblot.

Chapter 12: The Gaussian Distribution
Gauss, C. F. (1809). Theoria motus corporum coelestium in sectionibus conicis solem ambientium. Perthes et Besser.

Chapter 13: Stigler's Law of Eponymy
De Moivre, A. (1738). The Doctrine of Chances: or, a Method of Calculating the Probabilities of Events in Play. W. Pearson.
Merton, R. K. (1973). The sociology of science: Theoretical and empirical investigations. University of Chicago Press.

Stigler, S. M. (1980). Stigler's law of eponymy. Transactions of the New York Academy of Sciences, 39, 147–158.

Chapter 14: The Baader-Meinhof Phenomenon

Zwicky, A. (2006). Just Between Dr. Language and I. Language Log.

Chapter 15: The Rosenthal Effect (Pygmalion Effect)

Rosenthal, R., & Jacobson, L. (1968). Pygmalion in the classroom: Teacher expectation and pupils' intellectual development. Holt, Rinehart & Winston.

Chapter 16: The Matthew Effect

Merton, R. K. (1968). The Matthew Effect in Science. Science, 159(3810), 56-63.

Chapter 17: The Peter Principle

Peter, L. J., & Hull, R. (1969). The Peter Principle: Why Things Always Go Wrong. William Morrow and Company.

Chapter 18: The Milgram Obedience Experiment

Milgram, S. (1963). Behavioral study of obedience. Journal of Abnormal and Social Psychology, 67(4), 371-378.

Chapter 19: The Bystander Effect

Latané, B., & Darley, J. M. (1968). Group inhibition of bystander intervention in emergencies. Journal of Personality and Social Psychology, 10(3), 215–221.

Chapter 20: The Hawthorne Effect

Mayo, E. (1933). The Human Problems of an Industrialized Civilization. Routledge.
Roethlisberger, F. J., & Dickson, W. J. (1939). Management and the Worker. Harvard University Press.

Chapter 21: The Streisand Effect
Masnick, M. (2005). Since When Is It Illegal To Just Mention A Trademark Online? Techdirt.

Chapter 22: The Spotlight Effect
Gilovich, T., Medvec, V. H., & Savitsky, K. (2000). The spotlight effect in social judgment: An egocentric bias in estimates of the salience of one's own actions and appearance. Journal of Personality and Social Psychology, 78(2), 211-222.

Chapter 23: The Spotlight Effect Through Life's Stages
Lao Tzu. (n.d.). Tao Te Ching (S. Mitchell, Trans).

Chapter 24: The Sunk Cost Fallacy
Tversky, A., & Kahneman, D. (1972). Subjective probability: A judgment of representativeness. Cognitive Psychology, 3(3), 430-454.

Thaler, R. (1980). Toward a positive theory of consumer choice. Journal of Economic Behavior & Organization, 1(1), 39-60.

Arkes, H. R., & Blumer, C. (1985). The psychology of sunk cost. Organizational Behavior and Human Decision Processes, 35(1), 124-140.

Chapter 25: Decision Fatigue
Baumeister, R. F., Bratslavsky, E., Muraven, M., & Tice, D. M. (1998). Ego depletion: Is the active self a limited resource? Journal of Personality and Social Psychology, 74(5), 1252-1265.

Levav, J., & Heitmann, M. (2010). The effect of choice complexity on perception of time spent choosing: When choice takes longer but feels shorter. Journal of Marketing Research, 47(1), 182-195.

Chapter 26: Hick's Law

Hick, W.E. (1952). On the rate of gain of information. Quarterly Journal of Experimental Psychology, 4(1), 11–26. DOI: 10.1080/17470215208416600.

Hyman, R. (1953). Stimulus information as a determinant of reaction time. Journal of Experimental Psychology, 45(3), 188–196. DOI: 10.1037/h0056940.

Chapter 27: The Scarcity Principle

Cialdini, R. B. (1984). Influence: The Psychology of Persuasion. William Morrow.

Chapter 28: Fredkin's Paradox

Fredkin, E. (1986). Digital Mechanics: An Informational Process Based on Reversible Universal Cellular Automata. Physica D: Nonlinear Phenomena, 45(1-3), 254-270.

Chapter 29: The Endowment Effect

Kahneman, D., Knetsch, J. L., & Thaler, R. H. (1990). Experimental Tests of the Endowment Effect and the Coase Theorem. Journal of Political Economy, 98(6), 1325-1348.

Chapter 31: The Hedonic Treadmill

Brickman, P., & Campbell, D. T. (1971). Hedonic Relativism and Planning the Good Society. In M. H. Apley (Ed.), Adaptation Level Theory: A Symposium (pp. 287–302). New York: Academic Press.

Chapter 32: The Happiness-Income Correlation

Kahneman, D., & Deaton, A. (2010). High income improves evaluation of life but not emotional well-being. Proceedings of the National Academy of Sciences, 107(38), 16489-16493.

Killingsworth, M. A. (2021). Experienced well-being rises with income, even above $75,000 per year. Proceedings of the National Academy of Sciences, 118(4), e2016976118.

Killingsworth, M. A., Kahneman, D., & Mellers, B. (2023). Income and emotional well-being: A conflict resolved. Proceedings of the National Academy of Sciences, 120(10), e2208661120.

Chapter 33: The Kübler-Ross Model
Kübler-Ross, E. (1969). On Death and Dying. Macmillan.

Chapter 34: The Romantic Fantasy Effect
Festinger, L. (1957). A Theory of Cognitive Dissonance. Stanford University Press.

Knox, D., Zusman, M. E., Daniels, V., & Brantley, A. (2002). Absence makes the heart grow fonder? Long distance dating relationships among college students. College Student Journal, 36(3), 364-366.

Warhol, A. (1975). The Philosophy of Andy Warhol (From A to B and Back Again). Harcourt Brace Jovanovich.

Chapter 35: The Ben Franklin Effect
Franklin, B. (1791). The Autobiography of Benjamin Franklin. J. Parsons.

Jecker, J., & Landy, D. (1969). Liking a Person as a Function of Doing Him a Favor. Human Relations, 22(4), 371-378.

Chapter 36: The Hedgehog's Dilemma
Schopenhauer, A. (1851). Parerga and Paralipomena: Short Philosophical Essays. (E. Payne, Trans.). Clarendon Press. (Original work published 1851)

May, R. (1983). The Discovery of Being: Writings in Existential Psychology. W. W. Norton & Company.

Chapter 38: Parkinson's Law
Parkinson, C. N. (1955, November 19). Parkinson's Law. The Economist.

Chapter 39: The Yerkes-Dodson Law

Yerkes, R. M., & Dodson, J. D. (1908). The relation of strength of stimulus to rapidity of habit-formation. Journal of Comparative Neurology and Psychology, 18(5), 459-482.

Selye, H. (1956). The Stress of Life. McGraw-Hill.

Chapter 40: The Over-justification Effect

Lepper, M. R., Greene, D., & Nisbett, R. E. (1973). Undermining children's intrinsic interest with extrinsic reward: A test of the "over-justification" hypothesis. Journal of Personality and Social Psychology, 28(1), 129-137.

Chapter 41: The Zeigarnik Effect

Zeigarnik, B. (1927). On finished and unfinished tasks. Psychologische Forschung, 9, 1–85. (Original study conducted in German)

Chapter 42: The Red Queen hypothesis

Van Valen, L. (1973). A new evolutionary law. Evolutionary Theory, 1, 1-30.

Chapter 43: The Incremental Triumphs Framework

Weick, K. E. (1984). Small wins: Redefining the scale of social problems. American Psychologist, 39(1), 40-49.

Chapter 44: The Reflection Ripple Effect

Schön, D. A. (1983). The Reflective Practitioner: How Professionals Think in Action. Basic Books.

Kolb, D. A. (1984). Experiential Learning: Experience as the Source of Learning and Development. Prentice-Hall.

Chapter 45: The Reflection Ripple Effect

Dewey, J. (1933). How We Think. D. C. Heath.

Schön, D. A. (1983). The Reflective Practitioner: How Professionals Think in Action. Basic Books.

Chapter 46: Life's 3 Ages

Levine, M. E. (2013). Modeling the rate of senescence: Can estimated biological age predict mortality more accurately than chronological age? The Journals of Gerontology Series A: Biological Sciences and Medical Sciences, 68(6), 667-674.

Belsky, D. W., et al. (2015). Quantification of biological aging in young adults. Proceedings of the National Academy of Sciences, 112(30), E4104-E4110.

Grossmann, I., & Kross, E. (2014). Exploring Solomon's Paradox: Self-distancing eliminates the self-other asymmetry in wise reasoning about close relationships in younger and older adults. Psychological Science, 25(8), 1571-1580.

Labouvie-Vief, G. (2003). Dynamic integration: Affect, cognition, and the self in adulthood. Current Directions in Psychological Science, 12(6), 201-206.

Chapter 47: The Law of Truly Large Numbers

Paulos, J. A. (1988). Innumeracy: Mathematical Illiteracy and Its Consequences. Hill and Wang.

Chapter 48: The Wisdom of Crowds

Surowiecki, J. (2004). The Wisdom of Crowds. Anchor Books.

Galton, F. (1907). Vox populi (The wisdom of crowds). Nature, 75, 450-451.

Chapter 49: The Flynn Effect

Flynn, J. R. (1984). The mean IQ of Americans: Massive gains 1932 to 1978. Psychological Bulletin, 95(1), 29-51.

Flynn, J. R. (1987). Massive IQ gains in 14 nations: What IQ tests really measure. Psychological Bulletin, 101(2), 171-191.

Chapter 50: Dunbar's Number

Dunbar, R. I. M. (1992). Neocortex size as a constraint on group size in primates. Journal of Human Evolution, 22(6), 469-493. https://doi.org/10.1016/0047-2484(92)90081-J

Dunbar, R. I. M. (1993). Coevolution of neocortical size, group size and language in humans. Behavioral and Brain Sciences, 16(4), 681-694.

Chapter 51: The Comeback Mindset

Dweck, C. S. (2006). Mindset: The New Psychology of Success. Random House.

Minnesota Gophers. (2008, February 21). Heather Dorniden's Unbelievable 600m Race [Video]. YouTube. https://youtu.be/g9rUUz8cMDM

Chapter 52: Life is All About Wins and Lessons

Shaw, G. B. (n.d.). Quotations by Author. Retrieved from https://www.quotationspage.com/quotes/George_Bernard_Shaw